Waking Up in a Cornfield...

selected columns
by
Chris Cox

1999

Parkway Publishers, Inc.
Boone, North Carolina

Library of Congress Cataloging-in-Publication Data

Cox, Chris, 1961-
    Waking up in a cornfield-- : selected columns / by Chris Cox.
        p.   cm.
    ISBN 1-887905-13-8
    1. United States--Social life and customs--1971- 2. Cox, Chris,
    1961-   . I. Title.
    E169.04.C69   1999
    973.92--dc21

Michelle Lakey, editing
Bill May, Jr., cover design
Julie Shissler and Robin Ann Aylor,
book design

ii

Table of Contents

Introduction

Part I: The Married Years

"Moo"	3	Muddling Through	32
Sad Songs, Imperiled Mammals	5	Catfight!	34
Selling Out	8	Sports Fans	36
You Call *That* a Motor?	10	First Class Scout	38
The Friday Night Girls	12	Never Trust a Beekeeper	40
The Failed Pacifist	14	Making My Bid	42
Does This Sock Really Belong There?	16	Lassie's Trying to Tell Us Something	44
The $11,000 End Table	19	Your Pilot is Charlton Heston	46
Baby, It's Cold Outside	21	Ode to Coppertone	48
Baby It's Cold Inside Too	23	Rock and Roll, Salad Bowl	50
My Daughter, The Tramp	25	The Ice Cream Artist	52
Pssst! The House is on Fire	28	A Tough Transition	54
The Prodigy	30	Such Sweet Sorrow	56

Part II: The Birthplace of Del Reeves

Message in a Bottle	61	Triple Bypass	83
Beautiful Boys	63	"I'm Eating an Apple"	86
Lloyd	65	A Man in Uniform	88
Uncle Sam	67	The Nature Boy!	90
Elgin & His Amazing Plastic Snakes	69	Dear Cindy	92
Karate Kids	72	Death By Garlic	94
Misty	74	The Bad Attitude Club	96
Roadrunner	77	Child Star	99
Best of Friends	79	"Birthplace of Del Reeves"	101
An Expensive Raccoon	81		

Part III: Great Insights and Other Delights

A Map of Wax Cities	105	I'm Allergic ... No, Really	130
You Gotta Know When to Fold 'Em	107	Male Pattern Baldness: Let It Be	132
I Love You, You Beast	109	"Why Don't You Call Brooke?"	135
Waking Up in a Cornfield	112	Radical Youth	137
Changes	114	The Car That Ate Itself	139
Shower Curtains, Putty Knives	116	Requiem for a Clockmaker	141
Born Sinner	118	Suing Mom	143
Ooh, That Smell	120	Merry Christmas	145
Lucky Strikes Out	122	Beanpole	147
Does This Punishment Really Fit?	124	The Professor and the Bunny Slope	149
The Search for Faith	126	Wedding Pictures	151
Call the Man	128		

Acknowledgements

for James W. Cox
and
Margaret Crouse

INTRODUCTION

I guess there's just no getting around it—I was a very strange kid. By the time I was 12 or so, I was already infatuated with a number of syndicated columnists, including Lewis Grizzard, Russell Baker, Sydney Harris, George Will, William F. Buckley, and so on. You know, the usual suspects. How many junior high kids do you know who obsessively scan the op-ed pages every day after school?

For awhile, my affinity for these writers shaped my politics. Yes, I was a pre-teen neoconservative, in feverish support of a strong military, big business, and repealing the capital gains tax. Unfortunately, these are not major issues among the 12-year-old set, so my forceful convictions did not hold much sway in my eternal pursuit of a girlfriend. Peggy Reeves was a peach, all right, but she wasn't much interested in the trickle-down-economics theory.

A couple of years later, I began writing furious right-wing tirades for the Blue Ridge *Sun*, a small local paper run by Millie B. Richardson, an editor with a heart of gold and space to fill in the paper. My rantings were, of course, preposterous, but she ran them anyway and gave me my first taste of what it's like to be a columnist.

Since then, I've written all kinds of columns, including sports columns, movie reviews, personal narratives, and social/political commentaries for a number of different papers, including the *Alleghany News*, the *Watauga Democrat* (Boone), the *Enterprise-Mountaineer* (Waynesville), and the Asheville *Citizen-Times*. While my political sensibilities have drifted somewhat precipitously to the left, none of my political commentaries, from either the right or the left, made it into this book. Neither did the movie reviews, so Roger Ebert can rest easy for a little while longer.

So what does the book consist of, then? Most of it is sort of personal narrative, I suppose, the sort of columns that do not blend easily with the columns one regularly encounters on the op-ed page. There are columns here on the vagaries of married life, the pain of divorce, the exploits of an assortment of small-town legends, the travails of a professional wrestler, and the various and sundry misadventures of your neurotic host. With a couple of minor exceptions, the editors I've written for over the years have given me a fairly wide berth to write about most anything I wanted, and I think the content in this book reflects that generosity. Almost everything here has been published in one form or another in different newspapers, and, for better or worse, I've stayed pretty true to the columns' original form, which is just a way of saying that I haven't made many changes. Part of the challenge of column-writing is saying what you have to say in 650-800 words. It is not surprising, then, that some of these essays would probably benefit from more development and there are, I am sure, several glaring examples of writing here that just doesn't quite measure up. I can only hope you will find that these are exceptions and not the rule.

When I was first approached by a reader about assembling some of my columns into a collection, I admit that I had some initial reservations. After all, I had always considered columns to be sort of "disposable," like razors or lighters. Long ago, I came to grips with the fact that the best turned phrases today are going to wind up in the trash alongside the chicken guts and coffee grounds tomorrow. So be it. But during the process of compiling this collection, I can honestly say that I believe there is something of value in these pages, maybe a laugh or two, an occasional tear, and a smidgen of insight here and there.

If you like this book, maybe I can dig up a few of those old right-wing diatribes, so you can get the inside scoop on how the average 12-year-old felt about the SALT Treaty in the late 1970s. Now *there's* a book only Bill Buckley could love.

Part I: The Married Years

"MOO"

Though I am fond of animals, I must defer to my wife on the issue. She, after all, has been a vegetarian for 13 years and I still eat meat, including -- but not limited to -- beef, fish, poultry, rabbits, squirrels, swine, and whatever's in a hot dog. Just looking over the list makes me feel like a murderous, blood-sucking beast — worse than a beast, actually, since a beast knows no better. Then again, a beast doesn't know enough to appreciate a nice grilled salmon, either.

Beasts do not marry vegetarians and therefore have no example set for them on the matter of a proper diet and basic human decency.

Yes, I have heard the arguments of the carnivores, heard them all. "Animals were put here for us to eat." "If we didn't eat animals, they'd only kill each other or die of starvation." "If God hadn't meant for us to eat animals, he wouldn't have invented the Western Steer. Besides, who wants to eat at the Western Bean Sprout?"

Still, some of these arguments are hard to swallow, if you'll pardon the expression.

The one about overpopulation, disease, and animals killing each other seems especially bogus, and it's the one I hear the most. If you look carefully, couldn't the same case be made for cannibalism?

"I'm sorry, dear, but we're going to need to thin out the family this year. Now go wake up Patrick while I warm up the grill."

It's not that my wife tries to make me feel guilty about eating meat, though she occasionally makes small gestures which could possibly — though I'm probably just being paranoid — be construed as such.

For instance, she occasionally serves me fish with the head still attached, one morose eyeball staring up, fixing me against the chair as I prepare to dig in to its moist underbelly with a fork. The fish has a facial expression of resignation, as if to say, "Go ahead, eat me. I'm just a fish. My wife and kids will understand. There is no future in living your life trying to nibble worms off around the sharp part of a fishhook. It's a fool's game, and I lost. So go ahead, have your meal. Never mind me."

Suddenly, it occurs to me. I'm having an imaginary conversation with my dinner. I do the only logical thing a rational individual in my position can do: I put a napkin over the fish's head and proceed to eat. This way, I won't have to make any more eye contact with him or endure any of his pathetic facial expressions.

Another thing my wife likes to do, though I'm sure it's a

coincidence and not intended to make me feel guilty in the least, is to emit tiny mooing sounds whenever I have a steak for dinner. I'll be sitting there lathering up my T-Bone with A-1 Sauce, a serrated knife in one hand and a fork in the other, just about to cut the steak into bite size pieces, the knife poised to make first contact...

"Moo...moo."

"Will you stop that please?"

"Stop what?"

"You're making those mooing sounds again."

"Am not."

"Are, too."

"It's just your subconscious haunting you. Maybe you were a heifer in another life."

"Can I eat my steak in peace, please?"

"I give up — can you?"

I look at the steak, but it's not looking back. There is no facial expression there to worry over. There's only succulent meat, with rich sauce seeping down its sides. And I'm hungry. Ravenous. Ready to dig in.

"Moo."

I wonder how bean sprouts taste with A-1 Sauce?

SAD SONGS, IMPERILED MAMMALS

My wife pulled into our driveway the other day and got out crying.

Uh oh, I thought. Trouble at work. Or worse. Had I forgotten something important, an anniversary or birthday? My mind scanned and came up empty.

I came outside to greet her and help with the groceries. She was still crying. I tried to find a way to ask what was wrong without making matters worse. Somehow, it seemed like trying to sit down in a tub of bathwater you've let run too hot.

"He's not the Cadillac kind," she blurted.

I'm sure I stared at her. I could not comprehend a syllable. Cadillacs?

"It's a song on the radio," she said, trying to catch her breath between sobs. "It's about a truck driver. He's not the Cadillac kind. It reminds me of your dad."

A feeling of dread came over me.

"Have you been listening to that station in Asheville, 99-point-whatever KISS FM, the one that changed over to...country music?"

"Yes, what if I have? This one song just reminds me so much of your dad."

She broke into a new round of crying.

It's not that I have a thing against country music. If you ever stop by our place and look through our collection, you'll see records by Hank Williams (who is to Hank Junior what the original Coca-Cola is to "New Coke"), George Jones, Patsy Cline, Lefty Frizzell, and Willie Nelson among others stacked right alongside the Stones, Creedence Clearwater, REM, Nirvana, the Clash, and so on. At certain times, I like to cry in my beer as much as anybody else.

But my wife ought not get tangled up with country music. I hope this will not be construed as a sexist remark. For the record, she knows more about cars than I do, is far handier around the house, and is at least equally inept at trying to read a road map. I'm not talking stereotypes here, I'm talking sensibilities, and the simple fact is that my wife is not the sort who can appreciate a good cry.

Less than a month ago, I came home with a copy of the movie "Free Willy," which everybody had been talking about and recommending with much profusion. We had even become excited about the whole thing and decided to make a night of it, so we ordered up some Chinese carry-out and settled in front of the TV

5

screen with our chopsticks and Won Ton soup at the ready.

I popped in the cassette, fast forwarded past the "Free Willy" merchandising and other previews, and sighed with a feeling of general contentment, a feeling that, come what may tomorrow, there is still this tonight.

And then I heard a groan. It was my wife. On the screen were these really mean-looking men in a big boat pulling an even bigger net. Then we got our first look at Willy, the carefree whale, frolicking about in the water with his friends and family. The boat moved in closer. The nets began to surround Willy, to cut him off from the others. I felt the familiar sensation of being manipulated, but good. I was sad and I was angry. I wanted the boat to capsize and the men to drown. I wanted Jaws to come along and eat them all like M&Ms.

I heard another loud groan, followed by a series of gurgling noises, then something more sustained and intense. Yes, crying.

"I can't watch this anymore," she said. She hadn't eaten so much as a water chestnut. "I want you to take this out right now."

Then her demeanor took on a more accusatory aspect, which is to say, she turned on me.

"How COULD you? How could you rent a movie like this? How could you do this to me?"

I told her I was upset, too. I said that the men were not just bad, but rotten, for trying to capture Willy and tear him apart from those he loved the best. She said that if I patronized her again she would tear me apart from my senses.

I put the movie on "pause" and took another approach. I suggested that things might work out for Willy in the long run. Didn't the title suggest as much? After all, the name of the movie wasn't "Fillet Willy." (I didn't actually say this, though I thought it—if I had said it, I would still be removing bits of Shrimp Lo Mein from my fractured skull.)

I said that if we would just get past this initial rough spot, we, like Willy, might overcome and experience greater joy later. So humored was she by this remark that she closed up her container of Chinese food, deposited it into the refrigerator, and went straight to bed without another word.

Of course, I was too stubborn to watch the movie under these circumstances, so I ended up watching part of a Monster Truck show on ESPN. Though I suspect Willy eventually did make it back to safety—probably not before befriending a small boy and enriching his life, not to mention teaching a bunch of insensitive adults a valuable lesson—I'll never really know for sure, at least not first hand.

What I do know, though, is that sometime in the middle of the night, I stole into the kitchen and ate the rest of my wife's Chinese food as the moonlight pointed a bony, reproachful finger at me through the kitchen window. That, I thought, will give her something to cry about. Maybe Randy Travis can write a song about it.

SELLING OUT

We live with all kinds of shaky compromises. I usually get by with this truth walled up somewhere in the back of my mind, out of reach and varnished over with my day to day routine, which is, itself, the very sort of shaky compromise I have in mind.

Of course, as someone once noted, the truth will out. For me, this particular truth broke out with style and vengeance during my vacation, of all things, at the beach, of all places, earlier this summer.

It was a family vacation at Kiawah Island, about twenty minutes out of Charleston. This fact alone constitutes one compromise, since I was once the kind of idealistic young chap who would have cast a disdainful eye on such gaudy examples of opulence as the million dollar homes that are as common on the island as commas in a term paper.

Once, I would have been certain that my even being there meant a kind of affirmation of this capitalism careening out of control. I would have wanted the alligators to take back the island from the rich and famous, by main force if necessary. I would have been delighted by the idea of a wallet made from the skin of Robin Leach.

But then, one night, we took a spin around the island looking at these homes and I caught myself coveting — oh, how I did covet — and I found myself thinking about the people who invented the Pet Rock and the Pocket Fisherman. Some of these homes were probably theirs. Dad blast it, what could I invent? I wanted to cash in my principles like poker chips, sell out my punk rock convictions, and claim my piece of the action once and for all.

Do you think anyone would buy the Pet Seashell? How about the Pocket Shrimp Net? The Magic Beach Towel?

I could feel my sense of values being swept out by the tide.

Without even fully registering the implications of my actions, there I was, playing golf. I once despised golf, primarily because I could not stand golfers. Rude, pretentious, tacky, and insensitive, gobbling up the pasture land like plaid-wearing Pac Men, trampling squirrels and chipmunks in their flashy golf carts. I thought golf was symbolic of everything I could not stand.

Then I played. On my first drive, I killed a chipmunk. Well, maybe, I can't be sure. That ball went rocketing into the forest with a sense of purpose I have never known, never to be seen again, and I don't know what sort of damage may have resulted or what the death toll might be.

But I know this—I was hooked, so to speak. Since then, I have purchased my own set of clubs and play somewhat regularly. Worse, I plan to devote even more time to learning the game, perhaps even taking a few lessons from some tanned guy named Chip. Still, you may shoot me on sight if you ever see me in plaid Bermuda shorts.

You have to draw the line somewhere.

YOU CALL *THAT* A MOTOR?

I sure do like it up there in the driver's seat of a big yellow Ryder truck. What a tingling sensation of power! What a rush of pure brute force! What a view of other drivers, slinking by in their tiny aluminum matchbox cars — don't they understand how easily I could crush them if they were to get in my way or insult me?

My wife and I bought a house Friday and moved in Saturday, and we are both thrilled. She is thrilled because our "new" home is so much bigger than anything we've had before and because it has hardwood floors and a fireplace and because it is hers, by Granny; no more landlords.

I am thrilled because I got to drive the Ryder truck.

I come from a family of truck drivers. My father is a trucker. So is his brother. Not to mention assorted cousins and other miscellaneous kin. For years, I just didn't get it.

Okay, so you're making pretty good money. But you're stuck up in this huge rig all day long driving thousands and thousands of miles all over this country, delivering everything from furniture to flounder, eating food so greasy it won't stay on the fork, getting hemorrhoids and losing sleep, seeing so little of your family you keep snapshots taped to your visor so you'll remember what they look like and can keep their names straight when Christmas comes.

For years I didn't get it, but now I do. It's raw power, man. And it's child's play. The United States is just one big race track and the big rig is the beatenest toy on it. The interstate is your kingdom, the driver's seat your throne, the gear shift your scepter. You are the master of all you survey. You will go where you want. Who can stop you? Some dipstick in a Gremlin? Outta my way, weakling. You call yourself a motorist? You call that a motor? I'll show you a real motor. Now pull over.

Maybe it's the macho factor. When you're behind the wheel of a big truck, your masculinity is quite secure. Everybody knows that the macho factor is the main reason why grown men like to play with toys such as guns, motorcycles, and power tools. All are not too subtle ways of saying, "Look at me, I am a powerful man, strong and dangerous and not to be messed with. I could shoot you, do wheelies over your carcass, and build shelves on your forehead if I wanted. Because I am a man, and I am surrounded by manly things."

The other day I saw a commercial for some men's cologne — Brut, I think it was — and in it there was an attractive woman extolling the virtues of all things manly, among which, she pointed out, most certainly did NOT include poetry. Great. I spend a sizable portion of time in my job as a college English teacher trying to convince students that poetry can be, should be, a part of their lives and that it is not just for brooding girls dressed in black or effeminate boys who couldn't make the football team.

But the widely held perception that creativity is a function of femininity is hard to combat, and that is probably not the fight we should be fighting anyhow. What we should be saying is that there is balance in nature, and that boys ought to be encouraged to write tear-streaked poetry and that girls ought to be encouraged to climb trees and that 32-year-old English teachers ought to be encouraged to rent big yellow Ryder trucks and rumble down horrified highways with "Born to Be Wild" blasting out the wimpy moans of "motorists" left in the dust.

You call THAT a motor?

THE FRIDAY NIGHT GIRLS

They wanted to talk to Jerry Garcia. That was the whole idea. In case you didn't already know, Jerry Garcia was the lead singer and guitarist for the Grateful Dead, the very popular, influential, and now defunct rock and roll band. Garcia died earlier this year, leaving legions of fans in a state of mourning and rendering traditional modes of communication problematic. I mean, it's not as if you can phone Jerry, or write him a letter. What would you use as an address?

But the inconvenient fact of Garcia's death didn't deter my wife and a few of her friends from contacting Jerry. One Friday evening after dining out — and I'm going to guess that the restaurant may have had margaritas on the menu — this group decided that they wanted to talk to Garcia and that doing so would require something more, uh, transcendental than Southern Bell. So they ventured over to K-Mart and bought a Ouija board.

"Attention, K-Mart shoppers. There's a blue light special on Ouija boards for those who wish to communicate with the dead. Aisle four."

I, myself, have had very little experience with Ouija boards, so my views here may appear biased and uninformed. Of course, this has never stopped me before, but it's one thing to offend the living, quite another to offend the dead, whether it's Garcia, Thomas Jefferson, Attila the Hun, or my great uncle Reese. I guess this is my central point — I just don't think it's a great idea to tamper with the dead. How can anyone rest in peace when there are so many giddy thrill seekers paging them with Ouija boards, peppering them with inane, perhaps impertinent questions about the great beyond?

Most of these dead folks spent the best part of their lives answering dumb questions posed by overeager journalists and obnoxious, prying fans. Wasn't that punishment enough? One can just imagine what kind of questions they are faced with now.

"Uh, Jerry, are you really grateful now that you're dead? Could you say 'hi' to Jimi Hendrix?"

I'm sure my wife and her group had more provocative questions in mind, but I was nonetheless disturbed when they came busting into the house that evening with their Ouija board. One minute, I'm sitting there watching a basketball game and having some popcorn. The next minute, my house has turned into a scene from "The Exorcist," with candles, and chanting, and spirits flying around the house. Well, I'm not sure about that last part, since I remained downstairs while the Friday Night Girls, as they have since dubbed themselves, decided to take their little occult sideshow to the upstairs bedroom.

During the game, I did hear a few strange noises emanating from the upstairs bedroom, and I must confess that the idea that the ghost of Jerry Garcia might be present in my own house made the basketball game on television seem pitifully insignificant. Our dog, Russ, I noticed, kept raising and lowering her ears as she sat nearby on her blanket. Could she detect the distant whistles of the dead, or was it something else, maybe a rabbit outside?

After a couple of hours, the Friday Night Girls came crashing down the stairs, making wild claims that they had, in fact, talked to Garcia. They had discovered that Garcia was in heaven, not hell, that he liked it there just fine, and that, surprisingly, he had not been besieged with questions about the afterlife from other Ouija board users and was, in fact, a little bit lonely. I don't know, maybe his star-crossed fans were just afraid they couldn't get through or that Jerry wouldn't talk to them. I've heard it said that the prettiest girls are always home alone because all the boys assume they have no chance, so nobody calls. Maybe that's the way it is with Jerry.

In any case, the lines are apparently open. Give old Jerry a call. And say hello to Elvis. As for the Friday Night Girls, I understand they have set New Year's Eve aside to contact another spirit, maybe Richard Nixon, to see what he thinks of the new Oliver Stone movie. They won't be able to use the upstairs bedroom, though, since I've had it boarded it up. At least until the priest comes. Or Jerry tells me to let him out.

THE FAILED PACIFIST

My favorite movie as a child was "Willard," the heartwarming saga of a young boy who adopts a pet rat only to have his pet rat go forth and multiply to such an extent that the whole town is taken over by this tremendous sea of rats, who proceed to eat the adults, including Ernest Borgnine, who resembled my sixth grade gym teacher at the time and therefore richly deserved it.

A few years ago, having matured into an alleged adult, I watched the movie again, looking forward to the same thrills and chills, looking forward to seeing Ernie Borgnine devoured by rats. Only I found it just wasn't the same. I didn't hate my gym teacher anymore, and rats, instead of the cool creatures in my childhood conspiracy against the grownups, were just plain creepy.

All I could think was, the kid ought to get a trap. A little cheese, a nice tight spring and — ZAP! — end of movie, roll the credits.

Funny how your perspective changes as your complexion clears up.

I was reminded of "Willard" a couple of winters back when, one frostbitten January night, my wife and I were in bed on the brink of sleep and the tiny footsteps — no, not of reindeer — of a mouse registered above.

"Listen," my wife said.

"I hear it," I replied with a sigh. "Great. Mice. I'll get some traps first thing in the morning."

She shrieked.

"You'll do no such thing! That mouse is a guest in our home. Heck, he was probably here before we moved in."

"That would make us HIS guest, I suppose."

"You suppose whatever you want to. You are not to lay a finger on that mouse, do you understand me? Besides I think it's kind of nice having another pet around the house. Now Russ has someone to play with while we're at work."

I tried to picture our dog at play with the mouse. Couldn't conjure an image. Then I pictured the dog as a cat, and the picture came into focus for me.

The nights of January dragged on into the nights of February, and the nightly dance recitals in our attic continued unabated. Her maternal instinct perhaps soothed by the pitter patter of little feet, my wife slumbered deeply as I tossed and turned beside her, pondering the merits of D-Con and my odds of convincing her that

I had mistakenly bought the poison, all along thinking it was vitamins.

Then we began to notice an increase in the pitter patter, which I thought might be the turning point in my ongoing efforts to vanquish the mice once and for all. Surely my wife had seen "Willard." Surely she would be able to picture me as Ernest Borgnine covered head to toe in a quilt of writhing rats.

"You are not about to touch those mice," she informed me one night when I had dared broach the subject. "You are not going to kill somebody's brother, not in this house."

Suddenly I was Cain, turned against Abel. I must say that it was at this point that I just quite simply gave up. All right, I thought, so I'm sharing my home with mice. In college it was the roaches, now it's the mice. So what?

I was miserable.

Then, without warning, the turning point came. The mice decided to explore new horizons, apparently having grown weary of dancing the nights away on our attic's ballroom floor. In short, they had chosen to pack it on up and move to the suburbs, which included our kitchen cabinets, a couple of closets, assorted cracks and crevices, and even an old appliance or two.

Thus it came to pass that the heretofore invisible mice, so sweet and cute and cuddly in my wife's sugar plum visions of waltzes and tangos, began to make fleeting appearances around the house. Verily, I say unto you that our formerly benign house mates began leaving certain distinguishable traces of their presence in drawers and among our foodstuffs. Whether these were mere tokens of good will or a clear signal of their desire that we switch to sugar-coated breakfast cereal, I cannot say.

Then, one fateful night, the bough broke. My wife and I had just returned from a late dinner. When we entered the house and flipped on the lights, a mouse of goodly, cereal-fed girth fell, yes fell, from the ceiling above and scurried beneath our frantic feet for cover.

My wife shrieked, just as she had on that night not so long ago when I had offered to buy the traps. Only this was a shriek of a slightly different caliber. This was the shriek of a lapsed pacifist, a woman with murderous intentions and D-Con on her mind.

"Get the traps," she said in a low, but firm voice. "Go and get them now. The gig is up."

That is probably what Ernest Borgnine said, just before being eaten alive by those rats in "Willard."

"The gig is up."

DOES THIS SOCK REALLY BELONG THERE?

Every marriage has its own set of issues, and mine is certainly no exception. My wife and I have been married for six years now, and at this point I think it is safe to say (because she hasn't read it yet) that we have identified our key issues and that all the ones that involve her are legitimate and correctable and the ones that involve me are genetic and fixed for all time. In other words, not my fault, out of my control, beyond my ken, and so on.

She has little tricks that get me, little traps she sets. For instance, she says I'm argumentative. This is an excellent trap. If I say I'm not, then we proceed to argue about it, outlining our various points in the following articulate and thoughtful manner.

"Are not."

"Are, too."

"Are not."

"Are, too."

This intellectual chess match goes on for a few minutes until she is overcome with smugness, at which point she says, as grandly as William F. Buckley getting the last word in a debate on his own show, "Well, I guess that proves my point, doesn't it?"

Well, I say it doesn't. But, then, I'm being argumentative, wouldn't you say? Conversely, if I agree with her premise that I am, in fact, argumentative, she prevails again. A classic trap.

Okay, so maybe I have seen one too many of those lawyer shows on television. Maybe I do enjoy contrasting my ideas on the issues of the day with others. Isn't this called conversation?

"But you'll argue about ANYTHING," she counters.

Will not.

But if the jury is still out (oops, another legal metaphor — I think I felt a tingle) on this issue, there is no argument (what!) about the next: I am a thoroughly, perhaps pathologically, messy individual. I do not dispute it one whit. Some say it is a sign of genius. Then there are those that know me. I will not tell you what they say.

I say it is genetic. My father is incredibly messy. He was quite certainly messy as a youngster, and his messiness carried on through young adulthood right on up through middle age. In other words, he set his course early and never wavered. Even today, his car looks as if someone has ransacked it looking for stolen diamonds. Strewn clothes, miscellaneous papers, food wrappers, enough change in the floorboard to pay next month's electric bill — only the driver's seat is even partially visible underneath this avalanche of, well, stuff.

Inevitably, my car is similarly adorned. As is my desk, my closet, and anyplace else that might be considered my exclusive domain. This, of course, does not include anything which might be considered OUR domain, by which I mean my wife's, by which I mean the house, which is always too messy by her reckoning and not even a little bit cluttered by mine.

For the benefit of those out there who are beginning to feel twinges of sympathy for my wife, maybe because you have also been afflicted by a messy person in your life, let me just make this brief, but hopefully illuminating, point: Messiness is overrated. It is not, as you may sometimes suspect, a form of subtle communication. If someone leaves a sock hanging on the bathroom doorknob, it is not necessarily a hostile gesture. It may have simply been convenient at the moment, an impulse so universal and so awesome that I believe it is the single explanation for most of the messiness you believe is aimed at you.

You believe this messiness is an intentional affront to your tidy sensibility, when all it really amounts to is that we, the messers, actually only meant to place the sock for A VERY BRIEF TIME on the doorknob in question so that we could collect it later and put it in its proper place after we have dispensed with the more pressing business at hand, such as leaving the top off the toothpaste tube, the seat up on the toilet, and whiskers sprinkled in the sink.

In other words, we really meant to get to it later. In fact, we're still hoping to get around to it; I swear it, we really are. In other words, we have good intentions.

The fact is, we WOULD get around to it, eventually, just not soon enough to suit you. Messy people get around to straightening things up about once a month or so, depending on the severity of the pathology and whether or not we've lost something important, such as money or a small child.

I'm not even sure why this is an issue in our marriage in the first place. After all, on my wife's very first visit to my apartment, I had to clear a path to the couch, which I then had to clear off so she could sit down. While I was in the kitchen pouring us a couple of drinks, she found a partially eaten barbecue sandwich under a few scattered papers on the coffee table.

"What is this?" she asked.

"It's a barbecue sandwich."

"You're not planning on eating it, are you?"

"Why, do you want a bite?"

17

"You've got to be kidding," she said, turning pale. "It's green."

"Well, maybe it isn't ripe yet."

This is one of the primary advantages of living the messy life — finding neat, unexpected little surprises you thought were long gone. As it turns out, this is also one of the primary lessons of marriage: Caveat Emptor, let the buyer beware.

THE $11,000 END TABLE

I spent last Saturday doing something I thought I'd never do—I spent the day looking at furniture. Just a few years ago, if someone had said, "Hey, Chris, let's grab a six-pack and spend the day looking at love seats and coffee tables," I would have probably said, "Dude, you need to look into a change of medications."

As a lifetime renter with no sense of taste and no reason to suspect I'd ever have any, I have never given much thought to furniture. In my world view, good furnishing meant a strategic placement of rock and roll posters to cover holes in the wall and large tears in the wallpaper. When I had a date coming over, I'd exchange posters, swapping Van Halen for a nice romantic poster of geese flying into the sunset. Ambience, you know.

As for the actual furniture, my working definition of good furniture was anything that had four legs, hideable stains, and no hypodermic loose springs waiting to puncture an unsuspecting backside. I thought that lumpy sofas had "that lived in feel." Sofas with fabric depicting wildlife scenes, especially big game, had that certain "pizzazz." Plus, stains tended to blend in well with pastoral settings.

Essentially, all the places I've ever rented—with just two exceptions—have come furnished, and I was proud as a peacock with whatever came with the place. Ruptured bean bags, broken recliners, wobbly tables, chests with drawers that would not close all the way...you name it.

I knew all this was about to come to an end when my wife and I purchased a home. Just as a reflex, I tried to negotiate the furniture that was already in the house into the deal, but the former owner balked and left us with rooms so cavernous you could actually hear echoes resounding through the long empty spaces.

Still, I believed I had a brilliant and workable plan to furnish our new home, a plan which reeked of elegance, thriftiness, and just plain good sense: We would take whatever our friends and relatives had sitting around in storage. When my boss offered up twin beds just two days after we moved in, my scheme seemed to be coming together nicely.

Enter wife.

"I want you to look around in all the local stores for nice living room suites—I said NICE, do you hear me—and when you're finished, I want you to go to Asheville and look there. And I want you to go to Ethan Allen. If you come back with any piece of furniture with sports emblems on it, you may use it in the new apartment you will soon be renting."

So, on Saturday, with my wife housebound studying for an upcoming test, I ventured into half a dozen furniture stores in search of non-sports-related furniture. Immediately, I was taken aback by the lack of rock posters available and the absence of Kool-Aid stains on the fabrics. Didn't feel much like home to me.

Then I began noticing a trend in the prices — they were high. Four hundred bucks for a recliner. Nine hundred for a sofa. Three hundred for a coffee table (two hundred for decaf).

At last, I made my way to Ethan Allen. Nice pad. I parked my mud-spattered Toyota among the Lincoln Town Cars and silver Mercedes and walked inside. I was dressed in jeans, a tee shirt, and a denim jacket. I had two days stubble on my face and was about six weeks past needing a haircut. I looked like Jed Clampett gone to seed.

This is OK, I thought. They'll think I'm eccentric. Swimming pools, movie stars.

And I was treated like royalty. While the most elegant woman I have ever seen in my life was explaining all the configurations, possibilities, and nuances in the latest contemporary group, I sneaked a peek at a nearby end table, which was just about big enough to park a TV dinner on. Pretty little thing, I thought. Nice wood, too. Four legs and everything.

And it was on sale, too — marked down to $11,000. Get 'em while they last.

"Sir," the elegant lady said. "This particular piece comes in cinnamon, butterscotch, or hunter green."

"Did you have anything in a grape Kool-Aid?"

We eccentrics have a reputation to live up to.

BABY, IT'S COLD OUTSIDE

In the dream, I am huge. My head feels heavy, probably from the antlers, and I'm foraging around in search of food. Tree leaves, bark, I don't know; small game, maybe.

I am a moose.

At five in the morning I snap to, my bee-stung ears as crispy and seared as overdone tater tots. I can see my breath billowing above me like some miniature nuclear bomb, exploding over and over. I appear to be stuck to the bed. In her untroubled deep-freeze sleep, my wife has burrowed into my side like some misshapen drill bit.

Somehow, her feet are glued to my left leg. The bottoms of her toes feel like frozen peas, hard as marbles. Two thoughts come to me slowly, across my mind's tundra, taking shape out of the icy mist.

Our furnace isn't working.

I am not a moose.

It is Sunday, January 16. I was going to sleep in this morning, but I was up past one last night fighting insomnia. The harder I tried to get to sleep, the more wide awake I became. After an hour or so of thrashing around like a sea bass stranded on the beach, I finally gave in to the inevitable and got up, wandering aimlessly around the house.

No sleep, then. Well, that's what Saturday nights are for. I looked outside at the thermometer. Three below zero. The furnace came on with an ominous shudder, lazy and utterly reluctant, like a fat, spoiled boy getting up from a vinyl recliner to mow the lawn for an allowance he knows he'll get anyway.

With nothing else to do, I went back to bed until finally, sleep caught me unawares. Then, in swift succession, the moose dream, the awakening, the bitter truth, the sorry spectacle of a man half asleep steeling himself against **indoor** temperatures best suited for the preservation of a box of fish sticks. Why wasn't the furnace on? In disbelief, I fiddled with the furnace thermostat, turning it to and fro like a lock on a safe, thinking it might come on if I could just find the right combination.

Nope.

Then I wrapped myself in a couple more layers of clothing and ventured out to have a look at the oil tank. Of course, I had no idea what I was looking for. I guess it was more of a reflex, like looking under your hood at the engine when something goes wrong with your car. You know you don't have a clue, but it beats not looking somehow. Maybe something obvious came unplugged, something with a sticker attached that says, "Hey, moron, plug me back in and you'll be on your way."

There were no such stickers attached to the oil tank behind the house, but there was a suspicious copper tube running from the tank into the basement.

"Maybe it's frozen," said my wife, who was up now and developing theories. One was that it would be easier for a small tube to freeze than a large tank.

If you'd been on or about the premises of 59 Miami Drive around seven o'clock that Sunday morning, you would've been treated to the funny-in-retrospect exhibition of your beleaguered and frostbitten hero, blow dryer in hand, ministering to the aforementioned copper tubing. It seemed as futile and ludicrous as a severely balding man attempting to blow dry his two or three remaining strands of hair into full-bodied, non-receding ecstasy.

While I was outdoors giving a perm to a copper tube, my wife was indoors placing panicky phone calls to various occupants of the yellow pages, getting lots of indifferent answering machines and one guy who asked if we had a service contract with his company. He was like a bratty kid genius with all the answers to the test, taunting those without them.

After awhile, we got through to a man who informed us that what we were doing wasn't so silly after all and that the furnace would come back on anyway in a little while if we'd already pushed the reset button.

The reset button?

We scrambled downstairs to the basement and searched for this mysterious button, finally discovering it behind a secret panel. I pressed it and the whole contraption roared to life.

Thaw. After a couple of hours, temperatures inside the house finally returned to normal, feeling returned to my ears, and I fell into a deep, dreamless sleep in which I was neither human nor moose. It was marvelous.

BABY IT'S COLD INSIDE, TOO

See the man. He is hunched over in the kitchen, bowing before the electric range, which radiates through the opened oven door what little light there is, bathing the room with an otherworldly orange glow. He kneels before the range as though in some private form of worship, as if he were descended from some strange race of people who had, through the ages, praised Westinghouse, from whom all blessings flow. His hands are outstretched in a gesture of supplication; it appears to you, the observer, as if he is trying in some feeble way to embrace the small warmth escaping from the oven, to contain it in his hands and hold it safely in place until the night passes at last.

In another area of the house, the wife sleeps under layers of blankets so numerous that her body makes no discernible dent in the surface; it is an ocean of quilts. Her breath can be seen mushrooming in the air above her placid face, evidence that she is yet alive and has not been crushed by the sheer tonnage of blankets nor frozen solid as a swordfish steak by the arctic temperatures that prevail throughout the home.

Shockingly, close inspection of the bedroom reveals that the window is open a good four inches, even though it is 22 degrees outside tonight with winds so sharp that they make a Ginsu knife, last seen slicing a beer can on television, seem as dull as a Bob Hope Christmas TV special.

The man would, in a better, more just world, close the window and the oven door and crank up the thermostat to at least 65 degrees, providing himself and whatever tender vegetation remains alive in the home a fighting chance for survival, but he cannot. He is trapped in a Kafkaesque world of bitter compromise and recrimination. He is married to a masochist.

Decked out in bedclothes that more nearly resemble Ukranian combat gear than pajamas, tucked deeply beneath the aforementioned blankets, protected against the gale-force winds pouring through the window, the wife is in ecstasy. To quote the venerable K.C. and the Sunshine Band, "That's the way, uh-huh, uh-huh, she likes it, uh-huh, uh-huh."

Needless to say, it is not the way the man likes it. It is not just that hanky panky, in such conditions, is problematic (remember: Ukranian combat gear). It's that spring is quite a ways off, and even with the oven on full blast, there is not enough heat to bring feeling back into his fingers and toes. If you will recall that famous Masters and Johnson study on Americans' hanky panky practices conducted back in the 70s, one of the major findings was that people suffering from in-home frostbite who are also married to partners who wear combat gear to bed are less likely to engage in hanky panky than their non-frostbitten, non-combat-gear-wearing peers.

The man believes this is a trend that still holds. But it is the price he pays for watching sports. Loathe? Hate? Despise? Detest? All of these verbs are far too inadequate to describe the wife's feelings about sports. There just is no vocabulary that will do, no word that can convey the savagery. She hates television, too, but she'd rather watch forty-eight consecutive hours of "Sanford & Son" reruns than one minute of a professional football game.

The man? Well, in his economy, the Dallas Cowboys are one of the four basic food groups. For him, the fact that the government is on the verge of shutting down is of far less consequence than Troy Aikman's knee injury, which may keep him out of the Raiders' game on Sunday.

He snuggles up to ovens and toasters so he can keep current on such weighty matters and follow his teams' travails all year. Comfort is one thing, my dear readers, the playoffs quite another.

If, in your own romantic pursuits, you should happen to come across this man in some nice restaurant or theater, and he is accompanied by a toaster, do not attempt to apprehend him. Wish him a happy anniversary instead. Count his fingertips. If there are ten, move on to your table and your life and revel, my friends, in the miracle of love.

MY DAUGHTER, THE TRAMP

I guess it's inevitable. There comes a time in the life of every man when he finds himself in his underwear out in his yard at two o'clock in the morning shooting at dogs. My time came just a few short years ago not long after my wife and I "adopted" Russ, our collie. We found out Russ was a girl after we had already named her, because she would not let us anywhere near her for about a month after we discovered her sniffing around the perimeter of our yard for scraps of food. We began leaving a dish each day, always spending a few minutes trying to coax her closer.

A couple of weeks after we finally gained her trust and our new family unit began to jell, another thing happened. Suddenly, without warning, Russ was in heat. We realized this when, seemingly out of nowhere, strange dogs began showing up in our yard with these eager expressions plastered on their faces. We kept Russ inside while I, playing the role of the protective father, did my best to discourage this gang of unsavory suitors by hurling epithets (and an occasional rock) at them.

And they really were a mean and miserable lot. A mangy pit bull with a limp, a shepherd mix with dung- matted hair, a chow with what appeared to be mud smeared all over him...these were the MOST appealing of what must have been a dozen or more lovestruck mutts. Suddenly, I had a daughter. You hope and you pray they'll attract the nice boys, and then your dreams are dashed by a guy named Mongoose with pierced nipples and the IQ of motor oil. Not exactly Supreme Court pedigree.

That is part of what I felt. These dogs were the canine equivalent of Mongoose having come over to pick up my daughter on his chopper, only Russ's "dates" were making their intentions for her all too clear. You might say they were even flaunting it. Further, they appeared decidedly unimpressed by my display of paternal authority. I began with a firm set of instructions, which I felt were direct and completely clear.

"Now see here, dogs," I said, confronting them. "I will not have any of you laying so much as one of your grimy paws on Russ. Now leave this yard immediately before I phone the pound."

But no matter what I said or how I said it, the dogs did not retreat one step from their positions in the yard. I found that if I accompanied my tirade with a giant stomp in their direction, they would each retreat exactly one-half step, not one inch more. If I chucked a rock at them, they might even back up a couple of steps, but within seconds would resume their former positions. It seemed pretty hopeless.

The only strategy that made any sense was simply waiting them out. If it was a test of wills, by George, we were going to win. We would protect Russ and her virtue by keeping her locked inside with us, leaving the dogs outside to fight it out amongst themselves. Might as well put the bayonet back in the sheath, boys. Your amorous advances are in vain. Nobody wants you here.

Well, almost nobody. As it turns out, my dog is a tramp. She wheeled around the room in a whining frenzy, pausing once in each revolution to scratch at the door. She looked into my eyes with a look of pure pleading. My body flooded with shame. I was appalled. She wanted to be where the boys were. I saw reflected in her eyes unspeakable acts, innumerable partners, wanton disregard for the mores of her community or the reputation of her parents.

We decided to practice tough love with her, keeping her locked in the house all night no matter how bad her tantrums became. We played good cop, bad cop. I was the bad cop, calling her down when her fits were particularly obnoxious. My wife was the good cop, offering her jerky treats when her behavior improved. But it didn't matter. We were fooling around with nature, and we were destined to pay the price.

If Russ wasn't keeping us awake with her incessant whining, the pack of dogs outside were with their lusty howls and whimpers. I had to get up at six to go to work, and I was already exhausted from a previous poor night's sleep. I tossed and turned, put my pillow over my head, cotton in my ears, pills in my mouth, all to no avail.

Finally, I lost it. I grabbed my .22 caliber pistol and charged outside. I did not make time for trivial matters, such as putting on a robe or a pair of pants. I was going to shoot 14 dogs dead, and I was going to do it my underwear. Of course, I wasn't really aware of what I was doing. I was, like the dogs, acting on pure instinct, pure adrenaline, only I was armed and they...well, they were armed, too, in a manner of speaking, but not with .22 caliber pistols.

If the spectacle of a deranged man in his underwear brandishing a pistol made any impression on the dogs, they didn't show it. They might as well have been wearing those stupid little hats that say "No Fear" on them. I realized in about five seconds that I wasn't going to kill any of the dogs, unless they attacked me. But I had full intentions of wiping the smirks off their arrogant snouts.

I raised my gun about ten feet over the head of the chow and fired off a round. Startled, he darted back about five or six paces. Then he resumed his former position, as if to say, "Listen, buddy, you'd better kill me now — I've got more ammunition than you do, if you get my drift, and a heck of a lot more patience."

I fired my gun a couple of more times. I knew it was pointless, but my gesture had been so utterly ridiculous that I felt compelled to follow through. When I returned inside, I saw what I had been reduced to — a man in his underwear firing shots in the middle of the night to protect the honor of a dog who obviously wanted nothing more than to get it on with the entire neighborhood. She looked at me as if to say, "How pathetic."

The next day we made an appointment to have her fixed. You can imagine how she looks at me now. I just hope when she gets a little older, she'll thank me for saving her reputation.

PSSST! THE HOUSE IS ON FIRE

I am not the most romantic guy in the world, though I'm trying to improve. Why, just the other day I brought my wife an egg biscuit from Hardees. She was sitting at her desk at work just typing away, not expecting a thing, and in I pop, clutching a Hardees bag and sporting a big old goofy grin. You should've seen the look on her face.

I am not always so spontaneous, though. Used to be, my idea of romance was letting her hold the popcorn at the movies. No more. From this day forward it is my pledge, my solemn oath, to be as spontaneous as my wife, who, just last Friday night, was so spontaneous that she gave me a little surprise I won't soon forget.

I was sitting in the living room, having a little dinner and watching a frazzled-looking man on C-Span talking about rising interest rates, when my wife stuck her head around the corner and made a brief announcement. "The house is on fire," she said, in a voice so calm it tinkled in my brain pan, rolling around like a quarter on its edge waiting to land.

I don't know about you, but I firmly believe that there are at least a few things in life worth raising your voice over. One would be winning free tickets to see the Stones. Another would be if the current baseball season is scratched due to a strike, with the Dodgers in first place in the West. Yet another would be if the house was on fire. I'm sure you can think of others.

In about a nanosecond, this news registered and I jumped up (spontaneously), shouted (because I thought it was important that, under the circumstances, someone should), and ran into the kitchen, expecting to be confronted by a roaring blaze. I expected fire to be climbing the walls, eating away at our tacky wallpaper like some ravenous beast, lapping away at our plastic cookware and smiley-face cups (remember those?) like some big, blazing cow inferno licking a salt block.

In short, I was afraid the whole kitchen would be more or less engulfed in flames.

Fortunately, the kitchen was not on fire. But the toast was.

Yes, toast, that kind of toast, the kind you spread with butter. Sunbeam, Wonderbread, Kerns, you name it. Toast.

"The toast is on fire," said my wife, opening the oven door as the flames jumped through like fugitives who had long been waiting on the chance to escape.

"Shut the door!" I yelled. "I think she's gonna blow!"

Of course, I had no idea what I was talking about. What was going to blow? Was there a secret gas tank in our electric stove that Westinghouse hadn't told us about in the manual? Had we purchased a special brand of exploding toast, a brand marked "flammable" right under a picture of the Sunbeam girl?

I didn't know, but I wanted to cover all the bases. Heroically, I pulled my wife aside and looked at the stove as if to extinguish the fire with a serious expression. Then I gingerly pulled the door open once more. Yep, the fire still raged in that hellish chamber, the angry toast underneath black in the pan.

At last, I pulled the whole stove away from the wall and yanked out the plug, as if denying the fire access to electricity might do some good. At that moment, my wife, in a gratifying burst of courage, pulled me out of the way, opened the door again, and hurled a smiley-glass full of tap water onto the fire, the result of which was that the flames shot out at us even more harshly and the fire seemed to grow in its fury, as if my wife were insolent and deserving of rebuke.

It should be noted, to our eternal shame, that we had not gotten around to equipping our rented home with a fire extinguisher, for those of you out there who understand that the only real remedy for toast flaming out of control is a fire extinguisher. We finally managed to call on our vast intellectual resources to put an end to the near-tragedy — my wife remembered from an eighth-grade science class that fire needs oxygen. If we'd just keep the oven door closed, the fire would eventually die out from lack of oxygen.

I couldn't have loved her more if she'd invented the light bulb.

We held each other in the smoky kitchen, every ceiling fan in our home whirring madly, carrying toast-smoke out into the night air like a rumor. The smoke alarm blurted out its panicked cry until I ripped it out of the wall, lacking the intellectual prowess to stop it any other way.

"You know," I said, as we danced there, entwined by silky smoke-ribbons, "maybe we ought to look into getting an actual toaster instead of making toast in the oven."

Yes, brains as well as brawn. That's why she married me.

THE PRODIGY

My wife talks in her sleep. Just the other night, she appeared to be awaiting the arrival of former first lady Barbara Bush.

"Barbara," she said. "Barbara, where are you? Are you here yet? Where is the president? Barbara?"

This went on for several minutes. I decided to try something.

"Yes, honey, I'm right here with you," I said gently. "George, too. We're both here."

"You're not her," she huffed, and promptly returned to Snoreville without another word.

I guess it could be worse. She could be cooing things to Brad Pitt.

Though I'm not really sure I believe it, she says I talk a lot in my sleep as well. She says that I tend to speak with a strong, assertive voice, stringing together big words in convoluted, semi-coherent sentences. She says it's as if I'm making a speech in front of a Senate subcommittee.

I never remember these dreams, of course. But in fairness, neither does she. The dreams I can remember can scarcely be characterized as grandiose. In fact, if there were awards for the most boring dreams, I would win hands down every year.

Other men tend to dream of feats either erotic or athletic or (gasp!) both. They dream of hitting a home run in the bottom of the ninth to win the seventh game of the World Series, then whisking Sharon Stone away to Cancun in their private jet. They dream of winning the Nobel Peace Prize, then whisking Sharon Stone away to Cancun in their private jet.

I, in the meantime, dream of cutting up a zucchini for a nice stir fry. Some men dream of Jeannie. I dream of vegetables.

Once in a while, I do have nightmares. We might be out of zucchini, for example. Or I'll dream that I'm in school again, and it's the week of final exams, and I discover that I'm enrolled in a course that I haven't attended since the first week of classes. I don't even have the textbook, and I can't remember the teacher's name, and I don't have on any underwear. Where did that last part come from? Don't ask me — it's a nightmare, remember?

I have to admit that my wife has far more interesting dreams than I do, though I guess you could say that she wins by default if she has any dream at all that does not feature preparing vegetables for dinner.

The truth is, she has spectacular dreams. And vivid. So vivid, in fact, that when she wakes up she is sometimes convinced that the dream is reality that she has simply yet to discover. It's as if her dreams are little hints to her that something wonderful has been waiting for her right along.

For instance, about a year or so ago, she dreamed she was a golf prodigy. Please understand that she has never so much as picked up a golf club before in her life, nor had even the slightest inclination to do so, unless it was to tee off on yours truly for some unspecified violation. Nosiree, she had neither played a single hole of golf nor ever wanted to.

But, in her dreams, there she was, pounding the ball with alarming authority from tee to green. Her touch around the greens was supple, her command of the wedge and putter phenomenal. Her game was, in every respect, flawless.

She awoke a prodigy. She was absolutely convinced that she was heir to the throne of Jack Nicklaus. Nicklaus? Piffle. Nicklaus had never hit the ball so truly as had she in her dreams.

She couldn't wait to get out to the course and break par in her very first round. Somehow, I coaxed her into hitting a few balls at the driving range before we actually played a round.

"You don't know your own strength," I said. "How will you know which club to use unless you hit a few first?"

Once we were at the driving range, she teed up her first shot, took a couple of confident practice swings, addressed the ball, zeroed in, and whiffed like Babe Ruth chasing a nasty slider. Then she whiffed again. And again.

Pretty soon, she looked like an angry gardener trying to kill a snake. But there the ball remained, mocking her from the tee like a bratty child. You can't hit me, you can't hit me!

After a few meager adjustments, she soon did hit the ball. A couple of times, she even whacked it a hundred yards or so. But it was evident that King Jack would not have to relinquish his throne anytime soon. And it was evident that she would not break par in her first round. A few windows maybe, but not par.

"I guess I'm not a prodigy," she said.

"Maybe not," I replied. "But your dreams are still a lot better than mine."

"Yeah, and so is my golf swing," she said.

You know, reality really does bite.

MUDDLING THROUGH

It is just growing dark. I am in the kitchen leaning over a boiling tea pot, inhaling the billowing steam into my congested lungs. My head is stuffy, too, from a lingering cold I can't seem to shake. I've tried those medications, and, it's true, they all tend to clear up the symptoms. But they leave me feeling spacy, jumpy, a little unhinged — operate heavy machinery? It's all I can do to refill a stapler. Stapling has become an issue.

That's the kind of week it's been. Plus, my back hurts at the base of my spine, the Dodgers were swept in three straight by the Reds, O.J. Simpson walks, the lawnmower won't start and the grass is six inches high, the furnace smells weird, and the dogs have been acting funny.

Current events are lousy, in other words, and I'm standing here over the stove about to have some hot chocolate and just muddle through the best I can. What the heck, I'm thinking as I watch my dog Mike snap at something — probably a bee — through the kitchen window. At least all this self-pity will give me something to write about this week. People expect men to whine whenever we're sick. It's one of the things we do best.

Suddenly, my reverie is interrupted and my view of Mike's antics blocked by a piece of loose leaf paper with a single paragraph scrawled out on it.

"Read this and tell me what you think."

It is my wife, the new student, back in school to pursue a degree in the health services, worrying over a rough draft of her first paper. Worrying a great deal. Worrying us all, me, her, the dogs, the pots, the pans, the kitchen table — even the teapot hisses complaints.

Of course, she is going to be an excellent student, and this harshly scribbled paragraph in front of me now is going to be an excellent paper. And I am going to get over my cold, the Dodgers will arrive on time for spring training, and the dogs will return to normal. But just now, this confluence is too much for me, and my position as the English teacher spouse of the new student working on her first important paper seems untenable.

I sit down at the kitchen table and read the paragraph slowly, consuming the words individually like little morsels of food. Then I read it again. It is, indeed, a good paragraph. A provocative opening sentence, a clear thesis, good development, sound arrangement. It is coherent and unified, intelligent and unpretentious. I cannot imagine any reader finding it as anything less than a very promising beginning. I say these things, more or less.

"Really?" she says. "Or are you just saying that because you're my husband?"

I try to reassure her that I am being objective, but I don't think she's buying it. After all, suppose her introduction was awful—unfocused, offensive, incoherent, riddled with mechanical errors. How would I bring such news to someone just now embarking on a shiny, new career path?

"Go back. You're beyond hope. You are the worst writer I've ever seen, and no amount of remedial work is going to help you. We must erase these sentences immediately and pretend this so-called paragraph never happened."

Of course, I would never make these remarks to any student, but that isn't the point. The point is, people are bound to interpret—and misinterpret—the remarks of others. So, if I were to say, "I really think this is a good paragraph, but you might want to clarify your thesis and repair that comma splice in the third sentence," she might interpret that advice as, "This is the worst paragraph ever written; the paper is already clearly doomed."

In short, we all see things through the distorted lens of our own experience. We can't help it. Oh sure, we all have our moments of clarity, but are they ever fleeting. Mostly, we're in a haze, muddling through, trying to keep it together from moment to moment.

Then again, maybe it's just the medicine. Better stay off that heavy machinery.

CATFIGHT!

I like cat people in general, and I admire cats from a distance, preferably about three miles. My private research indicates that cat people and cats share the following qualities: independence, irreverence, indifference, unpredictability, and excellent hygiene. Admirable qualities all. Still, I am suspicious of cat people in a likable kind of way, and I am deathly afraid of cats, which has developed into a phobia over the years.

My friends maintain that I have a "phobic" personality, which I flatly deny, though I will admit to being uncomfortable with water, heights, small spaces, escalators, large gatherings, Saran Wrap, marching bands, and any album by Juice Newton.

And cats, of course. My fear of cats, I think, can be traced back to my fourth year, when I had the horrible misfortune of stepping on the tail of a psychotic, 40-pound beast affectionately referred to by my Aunt Lillie, with whom I was staying at the time, as "Little'n." Until that day, the cat was, to me, much more like a rug than a pet, since it never moved, never played, never exhibited even the slightest pet tendencies. A gray, shapeless, inert mass of fur, harmless as milk.

I had neither seen nor heard about the slain, mutilated bodies of the yard moles, gathered in a pile behind the house, sacrificial offerings to the great Catbeast, their tiny frames torn asunder, little mole arms wrenched savagely away from their torsos.

No, as far as I knew, "Little'n" posed no threat whatsoever. I barely recall ever seeing her move at all. But then, in an instant, I made one false step. And I was mauled. Had it not been for the swift actions of my courageous Aunt Lillie, who shooed away my attacker with a large broom, I might have joined the mole heap.

As it turned out, I escaped with scratches and a battered psyche and a "phobic personality," all of which means, of course, that I have an alibi if I ever murder anyone, such as a politician or a talk show host.

Headline: "Crazed Writer Found Not Guilty in Slaying of Sally Jesse Raphael, Defense Attorney Lauds 'Cat Scratch' Strategy."

It happens that my wife is a cat person, which I discovered on our first date, when her cat "Sam" backed me into a corner while she was in the ladies' room, powdering her nose. We were carrying on a conversation, the usual nervous, first-date chit chat, through the wall, and she could not see what was happening to me. She did not see Sam arch his back and stalk me. She did not see his curved fangs glint in the lamplight. She did not see me cowering in the corner, attempting to act as nonchalant as a 200-pound grown man can act when he's at the mercy of a murderous animal.

At last, she appeared.

"Sam, you leave him alone," she said, walking into the kitchen as if this sort of thing happened all the time. "Don't mind Sam. He's in a bad mood tonight. Last Thursday, he got mad at me and wouldn't let me come out of the bathroom for two hours."

As she walked through the kitchen, Sam sprang at her from behind, clutching her left calf and digging in vigorously. She let out a yelp. I just about passed out.

Later on I discovered that I could protect myself by removing my black jacket and engaging in a robust game of "bullfighter kitty" with Sam.

"Ole!" I would say, waving my jacket like a matador in Sam's direction, whipping it smartly in front of his face. "Ole, I say!"

This usually had the effect of sending Sam screaming for cover, most often under the couch or bed, where he would hide for hours, until I had forgotten about him, at which point he would take a swipe at a vulnerable ankle, and I would faint.

Eventually, Sam ran away, perhaps unable any longer to resist the call of the wild. I'm sure he's chowing down on an antelope even as you read this.

I guess I'll never understand what kind of personality disorder could provoke a human being to voluntarily have a cat as a pet. I guess I'll never understand the appeal of being trapped in your own bathroom for two hours because Sylvester had a bad day. But I do understand one thing, which I think is a lesson we can all benefit from:

Cats hate to bullfight. Ole!

SPORTS FANS

Jack and Judy are fans of the Atlanta Braves. Fans, as you know, is short for "fanatics," a term which may seem a bit extreme for describing followers of sports' teams, who, in their zealous devotion to their team, are known to spend whole weekends lumped up on their couches with chips and clam dip, the remote control their only means of contact with the outside world.

Clad in tee shirts emblazoned with the insignias of their favorite team, these fans' worlds turn on whether a rookie shortstop from the Dominican Republic can lay down a suicide squeeze in the top of the ninth with one out and a runner on third, or if an aging middle reliever can squelch a rally to keep his team in the game until the big sticks can start producing in the later innings.

When their teams are playing, the rest of the world stops and nothing else matters. That is the best way to determine whether someone is a real fan or just a casual, bandwagon-riding pretender.

Jack and Judy are real fans. I ought to know. I'm their son-in-law, and I've seen enough evidence to convince anybody but the Simpson jury that they are, in fact, actual fanatics, guilty as charged.

And I'm not complaining. I, of course, am something of a sports fan myself, and the fact that Jack and Judy are also fans gave us automatic common ground when I first appeared on the scene a few years ago. Perhaps the most difficult moments in a male's life are those when he is faced with meeting the parents of a female he has just begun dating. From the minute he walks in their door, he feels their steely eyes locked on him, inspecting him like a pork chop, grading him like a final exam, suspecting him of unseemly practices and untoward behavior. Though he is as well-dressed as he can imagine himself to be, probably in corduroys and a Western shirt and matching socks, it is as if he is wearing a tee shirt bearing the words, "I have come to steal your daughter's childhood and sully her reputation. I will stop at nothing to have my way with her."

OK, so it's a pretty big tee shirt, but you get the idea. Though I have experienced this kind of scrutiny in the past and was expecting it again when I met Jack and Judy, I was bailed out by the sight of a ball game playing on their television upon our first meeting. Within seconds, we were discussing burning issues such as the Braves' starting rotation and the weekend series in Philadelphia.

In the meantime, my future wife, who has an attitude toward sports that can only be characterized as hostile, stood by patiently for an hour or so of this sports chat, then retired to her room not to be seen or heard from for some time, the bottom of the eighth I believe it was. In short, my first meeting with Jack and Judy was so splendid that it almost killed the relationship in its cradle.

But we survived, got married, and had the wedding in the afternoon because the Braves were on a west coast road trip and wouldn't be on for a few more hours, thereby allowing Jack and Judy enough time to make it back before the national anthem.

After we were married, we lived in Boone, North Carolina, for a couple of years, relying on the telephone as our primary means of communication. During baseball season, the marathon conversations between my wife and her mother took on a bizarre, slightly surreal quality, as Judy made her best effort to balance the two things she loves most in the world (sorry, Jack) — the Braves and talking on the phone. My wife loves only one of these things, so their conversations were often frustrating for her as her mother tried to talk with her and watch the Braves at the same time.

It was as if she kept switching personas, from loving mother to Harry Carey, right in the middle of their calls.

"Yes, dear, I know your brother is working too hard, but he...wait, oh gosh..."

"What is it, Mom?"

"Avery keeps getting behind in the count..."

"Huh?"

"For some reason, he's afraid to throw his fastball."

"Mom? Mom..."

"Oh, I'm sorry, dear, it's just that your brother has got to learn to relax and have more fun. You remember when...DARN IT! Throw strikes, hold the runner!"

This could, and did, go on for hours. Jack and Judy could have bought their own franchise for what they paid on their phone bills in those days.

Now, of course, we're right here in town with them, and, now, the Braves are in the World Series, which means that any night, they may drop in wearing their Braves' tee shirts and caps, and we'll strike up a conversation on whether a three- or four-man rotation would be more effective against the Indians, and my wife can once again retire to her room, not to be seen or heard from until the last out is made.

FIRST CLASS SCOUT

As a former Boy Scout, I am equipped to deal with a variety of situations that the ordinary man might not be able to handle. For example, if you ever need someone to tie a sheepshank knot for you, I am prepared. Also, I can whittle a tree limb down to a point so sharp as to be able to pierce a marshmallow or a weenie, and I know how to properly dispose of human waste in the wild, though I will under no circumstances dispose of yours.

If you need instruction on any of these critical issues, drop me a line.

But one thing I could never quite master in my boy's life was the old first-aid gig, which, as you know, is central to becoming a whole scout, a candidate for Eagle. When it came time to earn the first-aid merit badge, I realized my destiny was to remain a partial scout—better than a tenderfoot, certainly—but never Eagle, never Eagle.

Oh sure, I could wrap a tourniquet on a dismembered plastic arm or an ace bandage around a sprained ankle. But then, one night, we were summoned by the troop leader. He passed out a bunch of sharp little metal things, all nice and sterilized and neatly sealed. He wanted us to prick each other's fingers.

There we were, huddled in the activity room of the First Methodist Church, a bunch of pubescent boys with bad complexions, dressed in starchy green uniforms adorned with gaudy badges, patches, and emblems. We were about to make each other bleed.

My career as a nonconformist blossomed. Bravely (because scouts must be forever brave), I informed the scoutmaster that I had a rare, extremely contagious blood disease and must not, under any circumstances, have my skin pierced and my lethal blood exposed to my innocent fellow scouts. I told him that I would, of course, be willing to risk my own life for the much-coveted first-aid merit badge, but I could not put my brothers in green in harm's way.

Fine, he said, you can still do someone else.

But I could not. I simply could not prick another scout. And caught off guard as I was by his suggestion, I had no other courageous excuses in my reservoir. I feigned a sudden illness and took off, hiding in back of the church behind some hedges until my mother arrived.

Thus flew away the youngster's Eagle. And I have yet in the intervening years to recover my bravery in situations involving the spilling of blood, either my own or someone else's.

Just the other night, my wife fell prey to that most hazardous of kitchen tools, the jelly jar. I was lounging in the bathtub, when she walked in, her index finger wrapped in a Kleenex. The Kleenex was soaked with blood.

Utilizing my keen, scout-honed powers of observation, I immediately deduced that something was not right.

"I cut myself on a jelly jar," she said. "I want you to look at it and tell me what you think."

"What I think," I said, allowing the tub water to rise to my chin, "is that if you show me that cut I'm going to pass out and drown."

"Oh, come on," she replied. "It's just a little bitty scratch. I think I may have cut it to the bone, but it's not all that bad. I'm a little dizzy, but I'm fine."

She was heaping contradictions upon me there in the tub. Cut to the bone, but not bad. Dizzy, but fine.

"What should I do?" she asked.

Calling upon my vast store of knowledge, I immediately conceived a two-pronged plan, startling in both its brilliance and simplicity.

"Number one, get it to stop bleeding," I told her. "Number two, call your sister, the nurse."

Eventually, we decided to go to the emergency room, where my wife received a couple of stitches and a splint (remarkably like the one pictured in the Boy Scout Handbook in the first aid section).

I drove her there and back without incident. When we got back home, I made a fire by rubbing two sticks together for her to warm her bandaged hand against.

I'm not a First Class scout for nothing, you know.

NEVER TRUST A BEEKEEPER

There you are in your office, working away as usual, except, today, you're not really there, are you? No, you're not. Because outside, as you push papers inside, nature is pushing insistently against your window pane, urging you, calling you to, to...get OUT! The blue sky: you want to climb a mountaintop and just swim in it, don't you? You want to get into a big red and green balloon and keep going higher and higher until, way back down on earth, your office becomes the size of Washington's eyeball on a new quarter.

Maybe your window is open, and someone down the road a ways is cutting grass. The scent is driving you mad. You want to play baseball, or plant a tree, or climb a beanstalk, don't you, Jack?

Because it's spring, finally, and the world is awake, and the deck is reshuffled, and you're back in the game with a new hand.

Sounds pretty good, doesn't it? Well, it is, mister, but as you fire up that Hibachi grill and lather up those creamy shoulders and thighs with Hawaiian Tropic, you better look out for those bees, because I have a news bulletin for you: bee stings hurt, and spring, whatever joy it brings to your hammering little heart, also brings the bees.

Lots of bees, many varieties, all vicious. The dreaded bumblebee, defying all the laws of physics with its enormous girth, mocking Orville and Wilbur Wright, a terror of porches everywhere, its calling card a capacity to sting you over and over. Or how about the yellow jacket, a particularly ferocious creature, known to travel in gangs and attack without provocation or remorse. (I may be making some of this up: I'm not sure, but it all seems real, doesn't it?)

At this point, many of you are no doubt entertaining second thoughts about plunging head first into spring, as well you should, unless you are properly adorned, covered head to toe with a bee-safe suit, or hosed down with bee repellent. Other readers may think these precautions rash, my assessment of the dangers of bees a tad hysterical.

But these people, I swear it, are the perpetuators of a dangerous and irresponsible myth — to wit, bees will not bother you as long as you don't bother them.

My very own grandmother, bless her, can be counted in this number. She was once a beekeeper, a pursuit which places her, I believe, squarely on the lunatic fringe, in the same league with the fellow who makes his living with his head in the mouth of a lion or that handsomely dressed young daredevil, Evil Something-or-other, who used to jump over canyons on his motor scooter.

You may call this behavior eccentric if you're so inclined, but, in my economy, eccentric means collecting tin foil, or having tacos and fruit cocktail for breakfast every morning, or opening junk mail. It does not mean getting stung to death by a squadron of Japanese hornets, or being decapitated by a four-hundred-pound cat, or plummeting three miles off a cliff on a Suzuki.

"Bees can smell fear," says Grandma. "You mustn't be afraid of them."

"Are you not afraid?" I ask.

"No," she replies.

"And you've never been stung?"

"Oh, yes, many times. But I've become immune. I'm no longer affected by it."

My Grandma, the Zen master, lord of bees.

Not me. Or my wife, who, somehow, exceeds me in her absolute terror in the presence of bees. Our marriage is based upon a few sound principles, not the least of which is our mutual fear of things that sting. Another is our shared fondness for pizza without cheese — as you can see, we're in it for the long haul.

My wife would drive a Lexus into a lake to avoid being stung by a sweat bee. Once, in the midst of a three-hour road trip, we discovered we had been tooling down the road completely oblivious to the large wasp creeping around the back windshield. She saw it first.

"Aiyeeeeeee!" she said.

We pulled over immediately, opened all four doors and waited. Waited. And waited. The bee would either have to fly away or die of natural causes before we would even consider continuing our journey. Between the two of us, we were determined to demonstrate to the bee that we had the stronger resolve.

Is there a lesson to be learned here? Yes, I think there is. Go ahead and enjoy spring, now that's it here, but keep your head out of the lion's mouth, and, for heaven's sake, never trust a beekeeper, even if you love her.

MAKING MY BID

I have an aunt who's big on auctions. She's always prattling on about some great deal she got at the auction, and her house is so overwhelmed by the stuff she has accumulated over the years, she may soon have to buy another house to keep it in. In effect, her shrewd shopping and sharp eye have her on the brink of bankruptcy.

She swears that auctions are the best place in the world to get great buys and that anybody in somewhat shaky financial shape would be crazy not to go to them on a regular basis. Of course, she always chooses her words carefully so as not to hurt my feelings.

"Hell, you're broke," she'll say. "You ain't got a pot to take a tinkle in, and here you go spending eight hundred dollars on a couch. A couch! I could furnish my whole home and yours too on what you spent for that couch."

Though I respect my aunt's counsel, I must report, in the interest of full disclosure, that she also believes professional wrestling is real and that space aliens are living among us, collecting welfare checks and many other forms of government aid in an effort to bring our country to its knees so they can take over and rule, perhaps even going so far as to shut down all auctions.

After all these years of her enthusiastic prompting, I decided to take my aunt's advice a couple of weeks ago and attend my first auction. What the heck, I thought. I had blown the whole budget on that couch. One good thing about furnishing your entire house with one couch is that the other rooms look much bigger with nothing in them, but my wife is not keen on this advantage.

So I went to an auction in search of reasonably nice furniture at cheap prices. I arrived a couple of hours early to look over the goods so I could make informed bids once the auction started. Bids! I was beginning to feel powerful just thinking about it. Pretty soon the auction would start, and I might actually make a bid. I'd become a player. I'd shake things up. I'd outbid elderly ladies on end tables and lampshades.

I found the entire pre-auction aura wildly intoxicating. I found myself looking at a smallish piece of furniture alongside a nice lady about my mother's age. We were both sizing it up, looking it over as though we were mechanics inspecting a malfunctioning engine. We were sizing each other up, too.

"Nice piece, isn't it?" I said.

"Oh yes," she said sweetly. "That would go so well in my

kitchen."

"I was thinking of using it as a TV stand," I replied, calling her bluff.

We circled around it. She touched the surface and ran her fingers along a tiny scratch in the wood. Suddenly, the piece seemed familiar to her, as if it had run away from her kitchen and ended up here, and now she was trying to coax it back home again with her gentle brushing.

"What do you reckon it's supposed to be?" I blurted out.

"I'm not sure," she said. "I thought I might put some place mats on it, maybe some knives and forks in the drawers."

Where would she keep her spoons, I wondered. Would it not be a good piece for spoons?

Finally, the players all crowded into miniature chairs lined up in rows in front of the auctioneer and the auction began. I had my eye on three or four pieces. I had no idea what to expect, but I was excited. I was like a poker player with a good hand trying not to let on too much to the other players.

I discovered a couple of things right away. First, people will buy anything at an auction. Perfectly normal-looking people were bidding against each other for torn posters of Olivia Newton-John and rusty kitchen utensils. People were paying top dollar for decals of turtles and broken binoculars. It is absolutely true that auction-crazed folk were fighting each other for the right to buy stuff you couldn't give away outside on the street.

Another thing I learned is that it's not a good idea to move during the bidding. I almost paid 50 bucks for a radio that didn't work because I reached up to swat a fly. The bidding in general was a study in mannered nonchalance. Indeed, it was sometimes difficult to determine when someone had made a bid. There was no wild yelling or raising hands. A nod was better, or a wink. Any slight gesture would do.

By night's end, I had come away with three of the four pieces I had coveted earlier. My aunt was right — she could furnish my entire home for less than I had paid for that couch. I guess I have to give her that.

But I continue to maintain that Hulk Hogan is a fraud. So there.

LASSIE'S TRYING TO TELL US SOMETHING

Bark, bark, bark...bark, bark. Bark, bark, bark, bark, BARK. BARK! Bark, bark, bark, bark...bark. BARK, bark, (bark), bark, BARK. Bark, bark? BARK!! Bark, bark, bark...

Know how to get a dog to stop barking? No, this isn't a riddle; I really want to know. How do you do it? We have the technology to put an entire set of encyclopedias and the complete works of Shakespeare on one CD-ROM the size of a coaster, but we can't figure out how to get an excited pooch to hush his yapping so we can get a decent night's sleep?

I don't think we're trying hard enough. I've seen my tax dollars spent on studies ranging from cattle flatulence to the flow of ketchup. Why not barking dogs? Maybe, if we put our best team of canine specialists — kind of a doggy think tank — on it, they will discover that getting a dog to hush up is simple. Maybe they will discover that dogs are easily hypnotized. Maybe all one has to do is read Italian recipes to them. Maybe their eyes will glaze over and they will hush until you say "Cacciatore," when they'll snap out of it and resume barking.

All I know is that we have to do something. I was moved by the letter to the editor that appeared in Monday's paper, a letter in which a lady complained of the incessant, maddening barking of two large dogs in a pen near her home. She said they barked constantly, day and night, giving her no peace. She had complained to the authorities, but they kept passing the buck (Surprise!) back and forth to each other, and she got no relief.

I know what she means, though from a slightly different perspective. You see, I am the owner of two large dogs (though presumably not the same dogs who have troubled the letter writer, since she lives in another part of town) who also rank barking at the very top of things they like to do, right up there with eating my shoes and sniffing things that you or I wouldn't.

Since my wife and I are now town people, having moved in from the outskirts to the urban hustle and bustle that is Waynesville, we have taken measures to mitigate our own dogs' barking nuisance. For example, in the evening we bring in our collie, Russ, who is to barking what the Rolling Stones are to music — loud and prolific. I have actually witnessed her barking for twenty full minutes at a fallen maple leaf, perhaps in an effort to frighten it from our yard.

Though I dearly love Russ, I would like to take this opportunity to dispel once and for all the Lassie myth. You know, collies are smart, brave, and so forth. The fact is, if little Timmy had been forced to rely on Russ to save him from the well, he'd still be treading water. Instead of going for help, Russ would have reacted in the exact same, swift way she reacts to any situation, either urgent or non-urgent. She would have positioned herself over the well, though not too close to the edge, and she would have barked at little Timmy as he called out for rescue from the murky water below.

In the Lassie myth, the collie's bark would have been a signal (perhaps subtitled on television) for Timmy to hang on, that Lassie was going to go for help and save the day. In reality, the collie would have barked at Timmy for hours, never going for help. Roughly translated, the barking would mean: bark, bark, bark, BARK, bark, bark...bark, bark, BARK.

Our other dog, Mike, is a hundred-pound mutt whose mission in life is to sleep all day while we're at work, then stay up all night howling at the train and barking at all things nocturnal. We try to be good neighbors by bringing him into the laundry room on these occasions. But in our house, Russ has seniority and has not caught on to the concept of "sharing space," so she gets free reign of the house while Mike is relegated to the laundry room.

But having slept all day long, Mike thinks three in the morning is dandy time for play — noisy play — and when we drag our weary bodies out back to rescue our neighbors' sleep from his glad tidings, he romps around like a billy goat on a caffeine binge. When we manage to drag him into the laundry room, lock him up, and slouch off back to bed, he rages against the door with his tremendous paws, often emitting a shrill whistling noise as accompaniment to this god awful percussion.

Our neighbors are rescued, but we are miserable. This is not an every night occurrence, but it happens frequently enough that we, like the lady in the letter and hordes of people all over the country who have been the captive audience of man's best friend, are looking for solutions.

Maybe Lassie will tell us. Well, what about it, girl?

YOUR PILOT IS CHARLTON HESTON

(Topsail Island) — I married into a family that likes to plan. They also like to talk on the phone. And most of all, they like to make plans while talking on the phone. Now, here we are on vacation, a time to set aside plans and phones and just concentrate on enjoying the fruits of all the planning and phoning that brought us here.

It stands to reason, then, that the main topic of conversation during dinner on our very first night out would be — ta da — NEXT year's vacation. That's right, more planning. I guess I'm just surprised that nobody called a cab and went back to the hotel so they could phone the restaurant to check in on how the plans were progressing.

Still, it wasn't the planning that was bothering me so much as the nature of the plans, which involved flying to Mexico. On a plane. Air travel. Big old jet airliner.

I have a phobia about flying. My earliest memory as a child is a movie starring Charlton Heston as the pilot of a doomed airliner filled with doomed, terror-stricken passengers in bright polyester clothes. They were all about to plunge into the Alps or the Pacific Ocean or some place, and there was nothing Charlton Heston could do about it. Charlton Heston had played Ben Hur and Moses. I figured, if Moses can't fly a plane to safety, who can?

Since then, there have been numerous movies about airline catastrophes. I tell myself that this is a basic human fear that has nothing to do with reality — after all, haven't studies shown that flying is much safer than driving and much, much safer than writing sarcastic columns about the militia? Still, as a nation, we fear flying; as an individual, I'd rather swallow knives at the carnival than fly from here to Greensboro.

What does it all mean? I have convinced myself that the fear of flying is really an issue of control. Or, rather, the lack of it. A car may in fact be a more dangerous mode of transportation than a plane, but at least when we're driving, we have some sense of control over our destination. This is a rare thing in life, the sense that one has some modicum of control over his destiny. It is almost entirely self-delusional, of course, but it is nevertheless a small comfort, and small comforts are everything when you're on a 747, and all you've got to get you through your flight to Mexico is a pack of honey-roasted peanuts and a bottle of vodka the size of your ring finger ("Yes, ma'am, I'll have 14 more of those, please").

So there we were at dinner, discussing next year's vacation plans, and everyone was excited (because they were making plans, you know), and my reluctance settled in like a fog, erasing all it touched. Then they remembered my fear of flying, and it became clear that some time would need to be spent coaxing and reassuring me that there was really nothing, after all, to be afraid of.

They elected to soothe my fears with inspiring anecdotes of air travel past.

"I remember the time we were in a plane and the landing gear wouldn't lock down," said one of them. "We had to circle around and around until we were almost out of gas and there was still no signal that it had locked down. When we finally landed, there were fire trucks and ambulances and sirens and emergency workers everywhere. We couldn't see them, though, since we had our heads between our knees in the crash position."

Thank you. Very reassuring indeed.

"I got caught in a storm once," began another. "It was so bad even the pilot thought we were goners. We were in that storm for over an hour; we couldn't see a thing, and the plane was rocking like crazy. I still can't believe we made it. Neither could the pilot. He ended up in therapy."

Excellent! Exceedingly soothing. When can I board?

There were various other stories involving storms, fuel shortages, engine failures, deranged pilots, and so on. I was stuck in a bad movie, surrounded by a tableful of Charlton Hestons. I concluded that I would ride a burro to Mexico before I would fly there.

How's that for a plan?

ODE TO COPPERTONE

I have a tan. Well, sort of. My face and forearms are brown, and there is a nice V underneath my neck, though the rest of my chest is pearly white. Still, with my shirt on, you'd never know that my tan is only a semi, and I've heard a few remarks from friends and family who, well, have never actually seen me with a tan before and are therefore somewhat taken aback by my brownness.

The truth is, I've never been much of a sun worshiper, never understood the appeal of heading out to the pool on sunbaked summer days to lie uncomfortably on beach towel-covered cement reading the latest Stephen King novel ("King Lear" doesn't quite cut it at the Rec Center) while bratty, red-faced grade-schoolers do cannonballs off the high dive in an effort to get the pretty blonde lifeguard's attention. If this is your idea of paradise, you're welcome to my spot.

I suppose I could have gotten a tan playing baseball as a youth. The only thing that blocked the sun's transforming rays from reaching my lean, lily-white frame was the dugout, for the simple truth is that I was, for all of my Ruthian efforts, quite possibly the most inept baseball player my county has ever produced. I couldn't run, catch, hit, or throw, though I knew all the starting players in both the National and American Leagues, as well as their career batting averages and strikeout ratios. And I knew how to wear a hat properly and how to chatter: "Hum, baby, throw him the hammer, hum now. Bust him high and tight, batter, batter, batter, SWING."

Apparently, this was enough to keep me on the team, but not enough to actually get me into a real game, thus depriving me not only of the opportunity to perform heroic feats in front of the hometown fans ("Cox fouls one off! He actually made contact with the ball!"), but preventing me from getting a decent tan as well.

I suppose I could've gotten a tan in the hayfields or gardens or tobacco fields, but I managed to squeak by on mowing lawns and the generosity (and occasional forgetfulness) of parents, grandparents, aunts and uncles.

Thus, in childhood, my skin remained the color of vanilla pudding.

Though I was teased incessantly by my well-tanned friends, time has evened things out a bit. I run into them now, and their skin has roughly — and I wish here to emphasize the term "roughly" — the texture of an old cowboy boot. They are thirty and look three times that, while I still get carded at Winn Dixie.

In fact, my wife coerced me into growing a moustache and a goatee because she felt embarrassed being seen in public with someone who looked, well, so boyish (I'm blushing as I write). Maybe she was fearful that someone would mistakenly assume she was my aunt taking me out for an ice cream. I don't mention this to my brown, leathery friends, even those who used to call me Casper.

So why blow it now? Well, for one thing, I've taken up golf, a sport in which there is no coach to remove you from the game regardless of how inept you are, which is a plus for me, since my idea of a good day on the links is making it through a round without killing anybody. And even if there were a coach there to remove particularly dreadful golfers, there is no dugout to put us in, no golf chatter to justify keeping us on the team (imagine: "Hum, now, putter, putter, can't make it, baby, hum now, putter, putter, putter, MISS!").

I guess I kind of like having a tan, though psychologists and doctors alike are probably appalled at my cavalier attitude concerning the matter. A psychologist would probably tell me that I am engaged in a futile attempt to compensate for my childhood failures, that it is too late to assuage those hurtful memories, that I'm an adult now and aware of the damage the sun causes, and that I should just snap out of it and apply the darned sunscreen.

Having taken all of this into consideration, I can only respectfully reply, "Clam up, Casper. Are you trying to blind somebody with those legs or what? Sunshine on my shoulder makes me happy!"

Then again, when you begin quoting John Denver, maybe it is time to come out of the sun.

ROCK AND ROLL, SALAD BOWL

I consider myself a rock and roll fanatic. For example, I know the lyrics to "Tutti Frutti" and insisted that, somehow, the music of Led Zeppelin had to be incorporated into my wedding, which was the most important day of my life, except for the time I saw Alice Cooper in concert.

Luckily, my wife is also a rocker, so we persuaded our brother-in-law to play a Zeppelin tune on his guitar as she marched down the aisle. We wanted an electric guitar, with walls of feedback and groovy distortion, but we also wanted to get married outside — in case either of us chose to make a break for it — so there was no place to plug it in. Still, I must say I was gratified — and somewhat soothed — to hear a familiar rock and roll classic instead of the "Wedding March" just moments before taking such a serious step.

I think my wife was happier about it as well, since she is not what one could call the traditional type. In fact, she had been threatening all week to break into a full-throated *a capella* rendition of "Woolly Bully" right in the middle of the ceremony if the preacher did not take out the business about obeying from the vows.

In any event, it turned out all right, though my grandma still hasn't returned my Led Zeppelin live bootleg cassette.

A few years back, when I was in high school, I even bought an electric guitar myself and formed a band — well, it was sort of a band. We had three guitar players and a guy who played Tupperware with a wooden spoon and a spatula and a colander for a cymbal. We called ourselves the Saturn Four — because we were so far out, you know — and flailed away on songs by Bob Seger, Lynyrd Skynyrd, the Eagles and the Troggs.

When we couldn't remember the lyrics to a particular song, which was always, we'd just make 'em up, which is a long standing rock and roll tradition we wanted to honor. We even wrote our own songs, including the unforgettable "Vampires and Cantaloupes" and the equally stunning "Rock and Roll, Salad Bowl," which was written by our drummer as sort of an ode to Tupperware.

We never made it big. In fact, we never made it out of our lead guitarist's basement. We came pretty close to playing at a junior high school dance, but made the mistake of actually volunteering to send a demo tape to the junior high school principal, who apparently saw little artistic similarity between "Vampires and Cantaloupes" and "Earth Angel," which, as he told us during a stern lecture on morals and good music, was his idea of real rock and roll.

Dejected, we returned to the studio. But the magic was gone. And a few weeks later, our lead guitarist wrecked his car and got religion, going so far as to burn his AC/DC albums and replace his Jimi Hendrix poster with an eight-by-ten glossy of Pat Boone.

So my budding career as a rock superstar stalled. No million dollar contracts, no sold-out shows at the Fillmore, nobody to pick out all the brown M&M's from the bowl in our dressing room, and no crazed, idol-worshiping groupies at our beck and call.

Oh well, like the man says, it's better to burn out than to fade away.

THE ICE CREAM ARTIST

As February winds down, it is time once again to indulge in that most masochistic of American pastimes. Yes, it is time to look back and assess the wreckage of our broken New Year's Resolutions.

There are many casualties on my list, and no survivors. Due to time and space constraints, I will dwell on just a couple, just to let you know that you're not alone out there.

I was going to be less compulsive this year. When I felt I had to be compulsive, because it is my nature to be compulsive and one cannot fight one's own nature all the time, I was going to be compulsive in a positive way. I was going to exercise compulsively, or write compulsively, or do compulsive good deeds.

Instead, I have become addicted to computer games, eaten about seven hundred gallons of Breyer's ice cream, and made inexplicable purchases from the Home Shopping channel.

I haven't gotten around to starting that novel, as I swore I would do last summer when I was in the process of persuading my wife that a computer was just the thing to put me over the top as a writer. Instead, I've mastered PGA Computer Golf, memorized all the puzzles on Wheel of Fortune, and piled up absurd amounts of cash playing Jeopardy.

I'm a winner. I'm a winner. That's what I keep telling myself. That's what I'm going to write my novel about, how a 32-year-old man found life's rich pageant in computer games, how the search for the Great American Novel turned into the discovery of the Eternal Quarter. Endless games, over and over, dessert before dinner, no curfew, perpetual recess.

I was going to tone up this year, as well, as a break from writing my novel. I was going to run twenty-five miles a week and cut out almost all the fat from my diet. That meant I would have to monitor my eating habits a tad more scrupulously.

You see, one of my eating habits is to purchase a half gallon of Breyer's ice cream, usually Swiss Almond or the perceptively named Heavenly Hash, give that ice cream a proper amount of time to melt just so around the edges of the box, then tear into it with a big spoon or maybe a soup ladle. I'm in the habit of scraping the melted ice cream from all four sides of the inside of the box until the remaining ice cream resembles something like a football.

Then the compulsive part of my personality kicks in, and I proceed to work away at the ice cream like some kind of crazed sculptor on a sugar buzz, which, in a way, is what I am.

When the ice cream is at last reduced to roughly the size of a goose egg, I begin to feel those old familiar pangs of regret, feelings of loss and bad faith. Fat grams reel in my head like an uncontrollable merry-go-round in a child's nightmare. I sit there woefully on the couch and look down at my stomach—a reservoir built by Breyer's—as if it doesn't belong to me, as if it walked in nonchalantly through the door, hopped up on my lap, and sat down like an uninvited and very pregnant cat.

I know I must hide the evidence. My wife is certain to find the ice cream egg in the freezer tonight. She will stroll into the living room with that superior look plastered all over her face like cheap makeup, and she'll say, "You ate all THAT?!"

Quickly, I devour the egg, tear the box up into little pieces, and burn it in the sink, setting off the smoke alarm and scaring the dogs half to death in the process. I put on a sweatshirt and don't tuck it in. I rationalize. We all deserve a little ecstasy in our lives, don't we?

Eating ice cream is an art, like anything else. So just think of me as an artist, perfecting my craft, suffering for my art. Yeah, I'm an artist.

A TOUGH TRANSITION

Here is the one essay in this book that has never been published in a newspaper. And yet, without it, the next essay is going to come as a shock, too much of a shock. In fact, when I sent the first rough draft of this book to my publisher, the reaction of Michelle, his assistant, to the next essay can only be described as incredulous. You see, after all these other essays on the vicissitudes of a marriage that seems mostly happy, the next essay deals with my divorce from a woman I am quite clearly crazy about.

I used to think that was enough — being "crazy" about someone — and sometimes, in weaker moments, I still do. But it isn't, not really. No marriage can ultimately be based on the heady, drunken rush of new love, because that incomparable buzz cannot be sustained on the same vertiginous level for more than a relatively short period of time. Which is not to say that it cannot be sustained at all, or go even higher from time to time. It's just that, after a certain point, his endearing quirks begin to drive you homicidal. After a couple years of marriage, if he slurps his spaghetti one more time, you are going to gouge out his eye with your salad fork. And so on.

But even these are fairly trivial observations. It will come as no great surprise to anyone who has ever been married — or possibly even in a serious relationship — that a successful marriage is based on an assortment of compromises and sacrifices, both large and small. Ultimately, the life of a marriage depends on each partner's willingness to bear the cost of these. That's what happened to us, and that is as specific as I intend to be, because some things are private and should obviously remain that way.

It is entirely possible to continue to love someone, yet not be able to live with the compromises the marriage makes necessary (or inevitable). Sometimes there may be a sacrifice you are simply unable to make, not something small, of course, but something that strikes at the very heart of who you are and what you believe. Now what are you going to do? Well, if you are anything like us, you probably live with this dilemma for awhile, hoping it will go away, hoping the irresistible strength of your love will move the unmovable object of your conflict. Don't the storybooks teach that true love conquers all, that people for whom the glass shoe finally fits are entitled to happily-ever-afters once their prince or princess arrives at long last?

Even people who know better, and that includes you and me, want to believe in the fairytale. Maybe that is why Michelle felt "betrayed" by the divorce essay you're about to read. It **is** a kind of betrayal. I'm sure both my former wife and I felt betrayed as well, not so much by each other as by the broken promise of happily-ever-after.

"I'm crushed," wrote Michelle, in the margin of the following essay. "All of these are so celebratory — I feel like I know you two — and now divorce! As the reader, I am just **crushed**...so unexpected!"

I am sorry. I really am.

SUCH SWEET SORROW

If marriage, as Woody Allen once claimed, is the death of hope, then what is divorce — the hope of death, any conceivable end to the inevitable and sometimes unbearable pain? Or is it death itself, manifest in a hundred different ways, both large and small? Is it a monument to personal failure, a symbol of your lack of resolve and character, a gaudy trophy of your poor choices, a scrap heap of busted dreams? Or is it another chance, a fresh start, an opportunity for growth and an occasion for courage?

Having recently gone through a divorce myself, I can say in my own case it was a little bit of all of these. Or rather, a whole lot of each. Divorce certainly is a destroyer. It is a bomb that blows to shreds your sense of who you are and what you have become. It is a series of land mines, going off in your face when you least expect, the shrapnel of memories searing your heart. Little remnants of you, barely recognizable in the wake of each blast, float scattered about the breeze like dandelion fluff; they are no longer organized around anything and thus take no form, assume no familiar shape. The center around which your life has been defined is suddenly gone, violently and utterly ripped away. It is as if someone has given you a jigsaw puzzle of your life, removed half the pieces, and still expects you to form a coherent whole.

Marriage has a life of its own, with a past, a present, and a future. Divorce obviously transforms the future, robbing it of its eyesight, but it also, strangely, transforms the past. A working marriage exists in a continuum, with time past and time future embodied in an endless present — you and your spouse move through life doing things, acquiring things, accomplishing things, but no experience and no possession has a meaning except as it reflects on your marriage and its evolution. You may think of the past, but always in terms of the present. Look at us then, and look at us now.

Divorce creates a radical new context for the past. Suddenly, old Polaroids of vacations and anniversaries aren't reference points — they take on the weight of historical significance. With no warning whatsoever, ordinary household objects become animate creatures, fluent in the language of loss, alive with symbolic value. This shirt represents that crazy day at the mall, when we got harassed by that sales clerk who looked exactly like an Afghan Hound. Here are the candles, half-burned and coated in light dust, which you loved to light on rainy nights. This is the drawer in which we hoarded coupons we would never use. This casserole dish, which has seen how many nights of meals, how many noble experiments (chicken pot pie, with oregano), how many washings and dryings? This window, which we looked out one cold February afternoon and saw a cardinal, its brilliant red color a frail complaint against the gray, overcast sky, and we discussed the end of our marriage with pretend matter-of-factness, like a couple of bad actors caught in the world's worst soap opera.

Separation is purgatory, of course. You are neither here nor there. You no longer have any sense of where you're going, and very little of where you've been. Was it all a dream? Were those years really yours? Do they count? On your hands and knees, you grope along seeking anything remotely familiar, something to see by in the all-enveloping darkness, any sense of structure or order. Friends, relatives, other members of the awful fraternity of divorce, try to help guide you through it. Letters, phone calls, visits, prayers, wishes. All precious. You're not alone. But you are alone, and your loneliness is a tangible thing, something you become aware of all the time. This emptiness is a basement flooded with grief, and you spend the first several months up to your knees in it, bailing, trying to save your house, trying not to drown. People want to help you — and they do — but you must do most of the work yourself. You find that you cannot escape the reality of loss. Rather, you must, for a period, soak in it, swim in it, absorb it even. You must endure the inevitable stretches of self-doubt and self-recrimination, as well as the sanctimonious platitudes of those who insist divorce has become too easy. From those lofty perches, what can the suffering of others amount to but a glib analysis of statistics. Now you're a number, a troubling trend, a symptom of deteriorating "family values," all your pain reduced to sociology and political bromides.

All of this you must survive, in addition to letting go, once and for all, of the life you thought you had and the future that life implied. You must learn to wear that particular shirt, and light those same candles, and cook in that casserole dish, and look out the window again, at cardinals, whose bright colors may affirm, on darker days, the possibilities of life, the outside chance that suffering may, one day, be suffused with sweetness and new hope.

Part II: "The Birthplace of Del Reeves"

MESSAGE IN A BOTTLE

Since I can't talk to you, I thought I'd write you this letter. I don't get to see you much, and I don't know if you ever see me anymore. The last time I was there, I fed you little squares of cantaloupe with a plastic spoon while your roommate moaned something unintelligible about a sweater. On the TV, an invention you once despised and now depend on for company or diversion, guys and gals in red-and-white checked shirts and dresses square danced. With the sound turned down, they seemed ridiculous. You didn't care; the cantaloupe tasted good, and the nurse said it was the best your appetite had been in days.

We lost you by degrees, like a flower blooming or the sun setting or rust collecting on a child's wagon. Try to watch such change and it stops, but look away for just a moment and it comes on you hard and shocking.

You were always a man who moved according to his own rhythms, a little out of the mainstream, sometimes a complete mystery even to those who loved you, but, all right, you lived by your own lights, with no apologies and no requests for help. This freedom you embodied was what I admired about you the most.

What a cruel mockery, then, this rest home, some stranger shaving your face and brushing your teeth and telling you how "good" you're doing when you manage to swallow a couple of bites of Jell-O. What a cruel fate, this Alzheimer's, which has robbed you of the one thing you cherished the most—your independence. Now you depend on everybody for everything.

I used to be in awe of you, afraid of you, nervous even breathing in your presence. You were, after all, a stern man and not much of a talker, though when the mood struck you'd spin a good yarn about your days traveling across the country, making music with your banjo and a guy named Howard, who played a pretty mean fiddle. You were gentle with your dogs, but it was said that you'd think nothing of tossing a new litter of kittens into the river. You'd put them inside a sack with a rock in it. Sometimes, I had nightmares about being trapped in that sack under water.

But you were good to all your grandchildren in your own rough-hewn way. You taught us about gun safety, how to hunt, how to skin a rabbit or clean a trout or get a tick off a dog's back. Mustn't be squeamish about it, got to be done.

I especially liked to watch you work in your shop. You fixed clocks and watches, sitting at your bench, stooped over with a magnifying glass studying the impossibly tiny machinery of time, setting it right. What can you do to fix time now? What is the difference between three and ten o'clock? Who are these people, huddled around you on your birthday, clamoring for your attention, brandishing cake, speaking in tongues? Will there ever be a gesture, a turn of phrase, some mannerism that can find a small groove somewhere in the impossibly tiny machinery of the mind and return you to yourself, or will you drift yet further away, all our words just messages in bottles?

It's come down to distance. As I sat next to you, only two feet away, I understood the gap between us was a galaxy, impossible to cross, and we had become two figures in a drama, unsure of our own characters, who we were supposed to be, what we were supposed to do or say, waiting on someone to give us some lines we could understand, or even remember.

BEAUTIFUL BOYS

I think Calvin had a crush on me, though it may just be that we had certain things in common that divided us from our rough and tumble peers there in the dingy halls of Sparta Elementary School in our fifth grade year. For instance, we both eschewed violence of any sort, particularly of the playground variety. When things turned ugly, as they frequently did in that maelstrom sometimes referred to as recess, when two young ruffians squared off over a girl who liked neither, or over an arm punched with a tad too much vigor, or over an imagined slight, Calvin and I withdrew, quivering like gelatin there on the outer fringe even as others drew closer in an ever tightening circle around the combatants, shouting oaths and encouragement. While others got their vicarious kicks, we checked our peripheral vision for any sign of a teacher.

In short, Calvin and I shared a certain effeminacy neither of us could deny, nor even hide very well. We were, after all, delicate creatures, thin as peanut brittle, wispy as smoke rings. Though we didn't look all that much alike, we were, if I may say, beautiful, with wavy, unkempt hair, luminous brown eyes and skin like churned butter; unscarred, unstitched, and—as yet—unblemished by even one pimple. Our school pictures were invariably flattering.

Even so, neither of us asked for nor were especially pleased with our lot as tremulous youngsters no one could mistake for being tough. There were, however, two key differences between Calvin and me. For one thing, while Calvin seemed to embrace his situation, I fought against mine bitterly, going out for the football team and despising every moment of it; lifting barbells in our basement at night after supper until my angel hair pasta arms grew limp; ordering Charles Atlas milkshakes out of the back of professional wrestling magazines. Calvin could be Calvin if he liked. I was going to be Blackjack Mulligan, with biceps the size of Butterball turkeys. If anyone kicked sand in my face, or said anything uncouth to my gorgeous future girlfriend, I would squeeze his head like a Florida orange.

Oh yeah...girlfriends. That was another thing that separated me from Calvin. While I had nothing remotely resembling a girlfriend in the fifth grade, I had an interest in the opposite sex that bordered on the obsessive, if obsessive is defined as an interest that occupies approximately 95 percent of your thoughts, and if approximately 95 percent of your time is spent immersed in thought. One day, as I sat outside the lunchroom completely absorbed in reflections on Mary Wyatt's new sundress, the principal happened by and took note of my studious demeanor.

"Mr. Cox," he said. "You are looking very pensive today."

Yes, that's it. I wasn't obsessed with girls. I was pensive. Good for me, and good for the principal for noticing. As for Calvin, he seemed to lack the same kind of covert enthusiasm for the opposite sex that I had. In fact, he appeared to be utterly indifferent to girls, even to Mary Wyatt's new sundress, which I found inexplicable. Of course, my own fascination with anything pertaining to girls, from the bra section in the Christmas catalog to my second cousin's underwear drawer, was as inexplicable to me as the random sprouts of hair under my arms that were as mysterious and miraculous as if someone had just discovered grass growing on the moon.

Most boys, I discovered, were nearly as obsessed with girls as I, and very few, if any, were as indifferent as Calvin. This crucial difference would ultimately result in my being somewhat accepted, at least on a conditional basis, by my non-effeminate peers, as well as a gradual, if inevitable, drift away from Calvin. If I'm ever feeling maudlin, I sometimes tell myself that I abandoned Calvin and feel ashamed for awhile. When I'm more in the mood to rationalize, I tell myself that it was simply a matter of changing times and shifting interests: suddenly, there in the fifth grade, I had an insatiable desire to look at girls; Calvin would have just as soon looked at pictures of a Praying Mantis.

I have lost touch with Calvin, of course. But I still think about him from time to time and the parallel lines our lives took through the maelstrom of childhood. I hope he's doing all right, wherever his life has taken him, and I hope he's found peace and acceptance.

LLOYD

When the phone rings a certain way late at night, you know what it is. Bad news. The worst. Coming across the wire like some ruined train on crumbling tracks in a dream that cannot be shaken awake.

It was about you, Lloyd. Said you had "passed away." Said you had collapsed while unloading boxes from a car. Said they couldn't revive you.

Those who announce death have a job, don't they? My mother announced yours to me in a voice suffused with pain, fear, and some brave calm. She said you were fifty-eight. Said you'd been to the doctor just last week and, though you'd struggled during the past few years with heart trouble, he'd pronounced you in pretty good shape under the circumstances.

I felt around in the dark for words. Finding none, I adjusted my socks. I believe I finally said it was horrible. I became aware of my own breathing, fragile as candlelight.

Later on, when I announced your death to my wife, I thought I sounded appallingly matter of fact, as though I were ordering a Big Mac and some fries.

On the long drive home, the things I thought about seemed impossibly tiny. You cooked one hell of a pot of chili beans. You were the first bald man I ever knew. The last time I saw you — a couple of months ago — you were up to your elbows in watermelon juice. We spit seeds into the grass. I said I liked cantaloupes better. You said watermelons.

You had the greatest laugh I've ever heard. It became your signature. People liked to come and warm their hearts by it, as though it were some little fire in a cold world.
During the funeral service, the preacher made note of it. He said he liked to think up jokes to tell you just to hear you laugh.

Now we come huddled around you once again, like small birds against a storm. You lie there in the new suit your wife, Ellen, bought you for Christmas this year. Your son and I agree that you look good in it. I mark how people touch you. One of your grandchildren approaches and rubs your smooth head like some crystal ball he'd like to see the future in. Your daughter keeps touching your hand. She moves her fingers lightly over the sleeve of your jacket, as if to fix a wrinkle.

But this touching is not strange. You raised a family of

huggers. We always looked forward to the holidays because we couldn't wait to see you folks, couldn't wait to see affirmed again the meaning of family, the abiding sense of peace and permanence that permeated the air in your home like a fragrance.

But now comes Christmas, and, with it, change. Some things persist, almost as if in counterpoint. The lights are up already, strung all over town in gaudy constellations, and people are cramming themselves into shopping malls in the usual feeding frenzy. Pretty soon it will be time for "Frosty the Snowman" and "The Grinch Who Stole Christmas," and pretty soon after that it will be time for sleepless children to begin marking off hours with uncanny precision and palpable impatience.

Then it will be time to go to your place, because that's just the way we always do it. The answer to the question nobody wants to ask is yes, we will be doing it again this year, and the next, and the next. Because we have come to understand the greatest paradox of our lives here on this spinning ball, that it is not just possible but certain that change and permanence must coexist.

We gather at these precious intervals both to measure change and to celebrate our victory over it. Yes, we're all a little older, a bit heavier maybe, or grayer, a little more or a little less of all the trivial measures that you can put a name to.

That which is permanent cannot be named. But it is real, and it is felt, and it is cherished, and it carries on beyond the grave. It carries your laughter back to us like the tide. It permeates the air like a fragrance.

Yes, we'll gather together this Christmas at your place, Lloyd. And though you'll be absent in one way, you'll also be right there among us again and forevermore, real and permanent in a way that can never be named. Because in this sad, old world where most of us put our focus on resisting change that will not be resisted, the most important things we have cannot be touched by time.

UNCLE SAM

My uncle Sam was the pride and center of the family. As a young man, he overcame a decidedly underwhelming score on his SAT and barely eked into Western Carolina University. He struggled mightily to keep his grades high enough to pursue his dream of going to law school, a dream that anyone who knew Sam casually in high school would have laughed at, not because of a lack of intelligence, but because Sam had a stuttering problem that bordered on the extreme.

Oftentimes, he had difficulty stringing together more than a handful of words before stumbling onto a word that simply refused to dislodge itself from his throat—his words were grinding gears, trying to click into place, trying to move on down the road, while nervous passengers waited, helpless. Determined as he was, the very idea of Sam delivering an opening statement or cross-examining a witness was nearly impossible to imagine. It was almost as if a person born with no legs had decided to pursue a career as a power forward in the NBA. Noble, awe-inspiring, but come on—get real.

Well, Sam got real, got over his stuttering problem almost completely, and made it through law school at Wake Forest, living his dream instead of dreaming his life. He married his college sweetheart, fathered two beautiful boys, established a very successful practice with his brother-in-law, and, for a great many people, restored their faith in the practice of law as a noble calling. If you're ever in Sparta and ask around, I guarantee that you will not find one soul who would utter even a negative syllable about Sam Evans. People respected him as a man of integrity and principle, and they knew they could count on him under any circumstances. In short, he was as decent a man as I've ever known.

And he had an enviable life. By the age of 36, he had a terrific home, a loving family, a future in politics (he was the local chairman of the Republican party), you name it—his life was a model, a testament to hard work, perseverance, and goodness. If he wasn't perfect, he was damn close. By his example, he lifted up those around him, including me. It seemed that no one begrudged Sam his good life because he was so manifestly deserving of it. It was somehow reassuring that someone of such strong character could also be so successful and so popular—maybe the universe could be just, and good guys didn't have to finish last.

Then, one sunny afternoon in May of 1984, as Sam was pedaling

67

his bicycle on the Blue Ridge Parkway in a valiant effort to shed those extra pounds that always seemed to haunt his middle, a bizarre thing happened. The cuff of his polyester-knit pants somehow became tangled up in the bicycle chain, causing the bike to seize up and send Sam hurtling over the handlebars. The first thing that made contact with the road was his head, and he was not wearing a helmet. He was rushed to the local hospital, then to Winston-Salem. As soon as we got news of the accident, the family gathered into my mother's car, and I drove us all to Baptist Hospital, in Winston-Salem.

Sam was hurt, we kept saying on the way, but he could not die, since he was Sam. That was the extent of our logic, and it was more than sound — it was implacable. Sam would not die, and we would all learn the importance of not taking people you love for granted, and Sam would start wearing a bicycle helmet, and we'd all go on wiser and grateful for God's mercy. Sam would not die. He mustn't.

And he didn't, not that night. But the next day he did. He just died and left us, just like that, with no explanation. Time collapsed. One minute he was having dinner with us on Sunday, eating too much dessert, the next minute he was pedaling a bicycle on the Parkway, and the minute after that he was hooked up to monitors and fighting for his life. And then, a minute after that, he was dead.

As the mourners streamed in a couple days later, I was standing in the dark outside his house holding those same polyester-knit pants in my hands. I couldn't think clearly. Even though Sam was Sam, he was gone. But here were his pants, tactile and inarticulate. I held them as if holding meant something, but I didn't know what. The world was mute, the moon a cipher.

I stood out there a while longer in the dark, then put Sam's pants back in the plastic bag with his shoes and shirt. A breeze kicked up, and I shivered. Then I went back into the house where people were all waiting, surrounded by gleaming trays of food brought in by friends and neighbors. Nobody said much, because there was nothing much to say. So we just waited.

ELGIN AND HIS AMAZING PLASTIC SNAKES

It is Thanksgiving, and I am standing out in Elgin's yard admiring his plastic snakes. Elgin is my uncle, and we almost always have Thanksgiving at his and Aunt Lillie's place in the strange, beautiful community of Vox, a "suburb" of my hometown, Sparta, NC. Their three-bedroom ranch home is one in a cluster of homes in an area inhabited mainly by relatives from my dad's side of the family. Sometimes we have Thanksgiving at my grandmother's house, which is less than a quarter mile up the gravel road from Lillie and Elgin's, but most of the time we gather at Elgin's, because he always has something to show those of us not lucky enough to be able to attend the family's regular Sunday gatherings.

Last time I was up, he had just bought a new van that he and the family intend to drive out West this summer, and the time before that he had built a flowerbed in the shape of a giant heart in the center of his circular driveway.

Lately, though, he's been on a reptile kick. Suddenly, his house is surrounded by plastic snakes, frogs, and lizards, all situated in gratifyingly matter-of-fact nature scenes. For example, near the large living room window, a three-foot green and brown snake is coiled lovingly around a piece of driftwood roughly the length of a fence rail, while, just around the corner, a pair of rubber lizards sun themselves on a tree stump salvaged from a wood-cutting expedition. Beside the garage, where a flowerbed of marigolds once thrived, a trio of frogs, probably ceramic, sit in a semicircle around a makeshift pond, as if poised to jump in if startled. Elgin is in the process of looking for some plastic tadpoles to help add some ambience to his pond.

Elgin is one of the best men I have ever known. He is my idea of the perfect Christian, humble rather than smug, one who models his beliefs rather than proclaiming them from the rooftops. He'll never hold his life up to yours in order to bring your mountainous sins into the proper relief. He doesn't practice what he preaches; he practices *rather* than preaches.

When I was nine or ten years old, I was terrified of going to church because, every third Sunday, the preachers would go into explicit detail on the elaborate horrors awaiting those of us not yet saved, how even the very young would be held accountable for their sinful natures, how you never knew when your time was coming, and how young flesh burned just the same as old. Frequently, I left the church feeling completely nauseous and deathly afraid, my head dizzied by the scent of seared flesh and the tortured screams of the terminally damned. One day, after a particularly jarring sermon during which the preacher got so enthralled in his vision of hell that his voice began to lilt rhythmically while his body swayed to and fro like the pendulum of some eternal clock, Elgin approached me as I leaned against the gate of the graveyard behind the church, looking out over the rows of tombstones, pondering my mortality. Why couldn't I go up at the altar call? Why couldn't I just give my life to Jesus and put an end to the agonizing pressure?

Elgin knew what was wrong.

"You don't need to worry about getting saved until you're ready," he said. "It's not for anybody else but you to know when that time is, and when it comes you'll know. Don't you worry about nothing." Then he pulled me away from the graveyard, back toward the land of the living. I rode home with him after church, studying him in close detail, as if to memorize all of his features—from his sharp flat-top to the architecture of ash at the end of his cigarette—so when I went to bed that night, those would be the images I would remember, and not the hellish images which had been drawn so vividly earlier. Maybe Jesus would save me later, but I needed Elgin to save me then, and he did.

Around that same time, Elgin taught me my first lesson about the hard things you sometimes have to do as an adult. Animals are and always have been an integral part of Vox community. There have been generations of dogs and cats running about through the years, harassing the chickens when they take a notion, letting them enjoy a moment's peace when they don't. Mostly, these are community pets, a little fatter than the average since they get fed at several houses instead of just one, and their diet usually consists of leftover chicken 'n' dumplings and such, rather than Purina Hi-Pro.

When I was a kid, one of the neighborhood dogs was a large, beautiful dog we called Red, ingeniously named for his long, shimmering red hair. He was a smart, gentle dog who could do more tricks than any dog we'd ever had in the neighborhood, and the entire family loved him. Unfortunately, he had the habit of chasing cars, and nothing anyone tried could break him from it.

One hot summer day, it finally happened. Red got hit by a car, which crushed his hind quarters and broke both of his back legs. We heard the yelp from the back yard and came running, only to find him in the middle of the road, whimpering and helpless, unable to move. My cousins, brother, sister, and I were hysterical, but Elgin would not let us get too close to Red because he said Red was hurt and might bite us, even if he didn't mean it. Of course, we were screaming for Red to be taken to a doctor, and someone even suggested calling for an ambulance, but Elgin saw what had to be done immediately. He told us to go to the back yard and he'd take care of it. We did as we were told, but in a few minutes I couldn't help but peek, and what I saw was Elgin pointing a rifle at Red. I think I cried out just as the shot filled the hot sky like a thunderclap, and when our ears stopped ringing, Red was no longer whimpering.

I was so stunned, I could not speak, or even cry. I thought Elgin would save Red somehow, and instead he had killed him. It was like discovering that Santa Claus whipped the elves. I ran over to Elgin, ready to unleash all of my grief and confusion on him. How could he so nonchalantly pull Red out of the road like that after having shot him? Then I realized that, in his own quiet way, Elgin was as distraught over Red's death as any of us, probably more so.

"Had to be done," he said to me. "Couldn't let him lay there suffering. He wouldn't ever have been able to walk again. You wouldn't want that, would you? He sure wouldn't have."

As usual, Elgin was right. Red would have been miserable crippled. It took me a long time to absorb that Elgin had done the only thing he could do, the only merciful thing that could be done. I could not have done it. I hadn't been thinking about Red so much as I had been thinking about myself. I loved playing with Red, and I didn't want him to be hurt. Elgin, of course, didn't want it either, but it had happened, and he had done what had to be done, and now he had to try to explain the occasional meanness of chance to a bunch of grief-stricken kids too inexperienced to comprehend anything much outside the boundaries of childhood innocence.

And now, all these years later, chance brings me here again, to Elgin's ersatz swamp. I love the snakes, love the lizards. Thank you, Jesus. Thank you, Lord.

KARATE KIDS

Lately, I seem to be finding myself around a lot of kids who have been taking karate lessons. I can't explain it; that's just what's been happening. Maybe it's a trend, what with the popularity of the Teenage Mutant Ninja Turtles, the Power Rangers, and so on. In any case, it appears that lots of kids these days are taking up karate, which is not only an excellent means of self-defense, but a superb form of exercise as well.

Be that as it may, I have come to the following conclusion based on my recent interactions with the karate kids: I wish they would just go back to being the sedentary, out-of-shape, helpless brats they used to be.

It's not that I have anything against karate per se. I've seen my share of movies with "Dragon" somewhere in the title; I even used to wear a cologne called "Hi Karate," though I wouldn't swear to that spelling nor am I certain whether this is the sound one makes when one is about to chop a cinder block in half or whether it's just a form of address—like, what's up, karate?

I've got no beef with exercise, either. In fact, I think exercise is an important aspect of child's physical, mental, and emotional development, and it is my belief that in our headlong rush to make sure our children have mastered advanced calculus and are fluent in several languages by the time they've finished second grade, we have forgotten the crucial role of exercise in a child's life. In other words, since I had to do those damnable squat thrusts when I was in grade school, why shouldn't they?

Still, I think this karate thing is going too far. And I say this not so much as a concerned parent—especially since I am not a parent—but as someone who has suffered the result of one too many "demonstrations" at the hands (and feet) of these miniature Bruce Lee wannabes. In other words, I am sick and tired of being kicked and chopped by the little monsters. I say this, of course, in the most loving, nurturing, and supportive way.

I think it goes without saying that children are compelled by parental law and sick tradition to demonstrate to anyone and everyone they see whatever it is that they have undertaken as hobbies. If little Sarah is just learning the tuba, you know you may look forward to a somewhat halting, sometimes terrifying rendition of "Stars and Stripes Forever" the next time you're over at the Johnsons'. And you can be certain that if little Archie is taking piano lessons, you will be treated to an unrecognizable, horribly mauled selection from Bach. Either that, or "Chopsticks." I recommend the Bach, whether you can recognize it or not.

But an assault on the ears is one thing; an assault on the knees, shins, thighs, and—I gulp when I say this—groin area is quite another.

The parents, obviously, are willing conspirators in this assault. Having reconciled themselves to the possibility that little Archie may never become a concert pianist, they are relieved that he has an aptitude for something, even if it is kicking the crap out of their friends and neighbors.

"Go on, Archie," they'll say. "Show Mr. Cox what you would do if you were attacked by a large man holding a weapon...Here, Chris, lunge at Archie with this spatula."

"Well, I should get on back to the office. I've never really attacked anyone with a spatula anyway, so I don't think it would be very realistic."

"Nonsense. You're not afraid of a seven-year-old boy with an overbite, are you? Now, lunge at him."

"Hi karate!!!"

"Archie, help Mr. Cox up. Mr. Cox?"

MISTY

We probably let her live too long. Nobody ever said so, but the unspoken truth was that we all hoped old age would take her in her sleep, peacefully, gracefully, without pain or disturbance. She was either 16 or 17, pretty old for a dog, and arthritis had rendered her nearly immobile. Toward the end, simply getting up off her pillow near the fireplace had become an ordeal requiring great effort.

Her body had become brittle and gaunt, no resemblance of the whirling dervish she had been just a few years earlier, carving blurry, jet-black figure eights in the yard as we stood by like barrels in a steeplechase. She would taunt us now and then, pausing to face off and lunge at us, but the moment we made to touch her, she'd be off again in a wild streak.

She was a mixture of cocker spaniel and poodle with dark black hair, not yet six months old when my brother's first grade teacher gave her to us as a "gift". I was in the eighth grade at the time, my sister in the sixth. It is important to get these details right, because it was the beginning of an era that would go on for 16 years, a generation.

The teacher had already given her a name -- "Misty." My mother and sister liked it. My brother and I despised it. It sounded like the name of a perfume or a prissy dog with an absurd haircut. I was concerned that the name might appeal to the poodle side of her heritage and prevent us from having the playful, rough and tumble sort of dog we had always dreamed of having around the house. I didn't want to spend all our quality hours together grooming and bathing her. I didn't want a pretentious dog, too snooty to get muddy with me or chase a ball into the woods or wrestle in the living room. No, "Misty" simply would not do.

So, in an effort to offset the negative psychological impact of such a "girly" kind of name, I renamed her "Brutus." My brother took to it right away. He was one savvy first grader. But the new name was less attractive to my mother and sister, who refused to go along and continued, stubbornly, to call her "Misty" throughout the course of her life.

We prevailed anyway. Within a matter of days, she would as soon answer to "Brutus" as "Misty," and her personality reflected none of prissy qualities I had feared. She loved to wrestle and get incredibly dirty. She even loved to play football with us, though she never quite got the hang of the rules. My brother didn't quite know the rules either, though, which made our "games" more like anarchy with a Nerf football. So what?

My mother had warned us in the days leading up to the dog's arrival that she would, under no circumstances, ever, EVER, be permitted to set foot inside the house. This was a non-negotiable condition of getting a dog which we reluctantly had to accept and which prevailed for approximately three days after the dog arrived, until her nights of forlorn crying broke Mom's resolve, and she granted the dog a spot in the utility room. From there, of course, it was only a matter of time before the entire house would become her domain.

If you have ever owned a pet, you know the rest. She became a member of the family, not in any abstract sense. It was absolute. She ate with us, slept with us, and shared our successes and failures. If one of our hearts was broken, so was hers. If one of us was afraid, so was she. But she would not allow any of us to be lonely, even when we thought that was what we wanted, needed, or maybe even deserved. She had an uncanny knack for knowing just the right moment to jump up on our beds or on our laps. If you believe dogs lack real empathy, that's your problem. I'm telling you that she knew, she felt, and she understood.

She also had a personality as distinct as any person's, replete with quirks. There were certain parts of the house she did not like, certain times of the day she did not want to be bothered. She hated getting her hair cut and was embarrassed for days afterward, especially if it was a short haircut. She'd slink around like a ten-year-old boy who got caught cheating on a test.

And so on. We lived like that for awhile, and then a funny thing happened. We grew up and she grew older, faster than we did. We moved out of the house and onto other stages in our lives, and she stayed behind and began to deteriorate, rarely doing any sort of running, rarely even leaving the house. She began to get arthritis and her vision began to fail. Still, she lingered, unwilling as us, it seemed, to let go.

And so the day finally came. My brother and I drove up from out of town and took her to the veterinarian. We didn't talk much on the drive over and none at all in the waiting room. Our pain was a fog in the room.

We buried her in a backyard thick with memories. No one spoke. There were no words to articulate this loss, this letting go. We all knew, I think, that we were not just burying a member of the family, but closing the book on a significant chapter of our lives. It had already been written, and there was no more writing to be done there.

Every few moments, as we stood there locked in our bond of silence, I thought I saw a blurry, black streak out of the corner of my eye. In the few years since, that sensation hasn't gone away. I guess it never will.

ROADRUNNER

Even in the early days, Roadrunner was a physical marvel, with goose egg biceps, wide shoulders, and a thick chest. All the time, kids would say, "Hey, Road, show us your muscles," and Greg (his real name) would smile shyly, pull up his sleeve, and flex. We might as well have been looking at the pyramids, for all the awe it inspired among those of us whose arms and legs were not discernibly more developed than the skeleton which hung like some bizarre Christmas ornament in Mrs. Estep's anatomy classroom.

One of only a handful of black students at Sparta Elementary School, Roadrunner got his name for his terrific speed, which took on mythic proportions by the time we reached the sixth grade. The school's annual track and field day became a joke, Greg's joke, his personal showcase. He won everything from the long jump to the softball throw, setting records and leaving the rest of us to munch on cartoonish clouds of dust. He was the Roadrunner, and we were Wile E. Coyotes, every one of us.

In those days, perhaps because I had grown up in a home mercifully free from the racist indoctrination so many kids must endure, Greg's blackness was no more significant to me than any other unusual distinguishing physical characteristic. At Sparta Elementary, we had red-headed twin sisters, a guy with a scar over his lip, and another guy with a wooden leg. And we had six black kids. Everybody else looked more or less the same, some a little bigger, some a little smaller—nothing that would stand out in a crowd.

Sure, I had heard quite a bit of racist talk, including that of a relative I always dreaded seeing who favored jokes about "jungle bunnies" and "spooks," though he'd go ahead and use the "N" word when he wasn't feeling especially generous. And I had even heard talk that blacks were faster and more athletic, but not as smart as white people and far more apt to be lazy or criminally inclined. None of this really took root in my consciousness, however, since what I heard didn't match up well with my experience. Roadrunner was athletic all right, but he was far from dumb. He could be lazy, but if it came to a contest, I had him trumped three times over. If there had been a field day for laziness, I would have shattered records in every event, and I was as white as your mother's china. Then there was Melvin, another black kid in our class. In a one-hundred-yard dash, I would not have bet on Melvin to outrun a California Banana

Slug. Since the stereotypes so seldom fit, I just dismissed them and went about my business, which was rebellion (Roadrunner and I shared a delicious anti-authoritarian impulse, which made us fast friends, even though I was no more athletically inclined than your average block of cheese).

In high school, math and hormones combined to change the world. My classmates and I became "young adults." We got girlfriends, held hands in the hall, kissed underneath the stairs going down to the locker room, wore each other's rings, made promises we thought we'd keep forever. When the rumors started spreading that Roadrunner was dating a new girl named Susan, there was a palpable tension in the school's atmosphere that I'd never felt before. It reminded me of the way animals behave before the storm comes, twitchy and alarmed.

Susan was a pretty girl, and she was a white girl. Even people who had always liked Greg said that he shouldn't be dating white girls, that blacks and whites shouldn't mix THAT way, that he ought to stay with his own kind when it came to dating. His "own kind," of course, consisted of exactly one girl in our class, who happened to be his cousin. But nobody bothered with the math. Instead, vague threats were made, though no would-be segregationist ever went so far as to make them specific, since Greg would have beaten him senseless for his trouble. Still, even though Greg feared no one, not man or beast, he must have sensed the very real danger his behavior posed, and before long, his relationship with Susan became invisible to the naked eye. If he saw her at all, it was never in public. If you asked him about it, he shrugged it off and changed the subject. There was an aura of shame around the entire affair that even the larger-than-life Roadrunner seemed diminished by. And it diminished us all.

I don't see Roadrunner much anymore, though I still get reports from my sister. A few years ago, he became involved in a pool-room brawl with a couple of local toughs and put one in the hospital for a lengthy stay. Mostly, though, he avoids trouble and goes about his business. The last time I saw him, we were in a tavern shooting a game of pool over a couple of Michelobs, and the conversation turned to the past, as it usually does among old friends when they've had a drink or two.

We talked about football, detention hall, and lost weekends. But we didn't talk about Susan. She never came up.

BEST OF FRIENDS

Stewart and I are like brothers, though it wasn't always so. When we were about seven years old, he once punched me in the nose at 4-H Camp over a disagreement about a tetherball score. The counselors said I was brave not to have fought back, when in truth I didn't know how to fight back. Stewart's father was a rough, ill-tempered man who taught him to hit first and ask questions later. My father was a generous, kind-hearted man whom I rarely saw, since his truck-driving job took him everywhere but home. My most salient childhood memory of my father is him kissing me good-bye, his face stubbled and splashed with Old Spice.

I've always been afraid to ask Stewart about his most enduring memory of his father. One day, about five years ago, his father called him on the phone and shot himself in the head while Stewart listened. His way of saying good-bye, I guess. Hit first and ask questions later.

Stewart and I didn't run in the same crowd during our school years. I tended toward the college prep kids, while he was more comfortable in the shop classes, among scruffy, vulgar boys who prized their jacked-up Chevelles above all other things. I was too wild for my crowd, Stewart too smart for his. But our school was small, so we went with what we knew, rarely crossing paths and going our separate ways at graduation: me, to college in Raleigh; Stewart, to work on the farm.

My first stint in college was an unmitigated disaster. I lived it up, lapped it up, experimented with various altered states of consciousness among new friends from distant, exotic places like New Jersey, who brought with them exotic devices and substances I had never seen and never tried, things which, in any case, were more interesting than my pre-law classes. In less than two years, I was back in my parents' basement, trying to figure out what had happened to my future, which was once so bright it was almost tangible, like a ribbon at the finish line. Now, I had not only lost sight of the ribbon, I couldn't even find the track.

Then, I found Stewart. One night, at a local tavern, we sat at different tables sipping our draft beers in silence, withdrawn and unaware of each other, a couple of characters damaged by collisions with the real world. Finally, he recognized me.

"What are you doing here, college boy?" he said, genuinely surprised. "Shouldn't you be reading a book?"

He sat down, and we talked. And talked. We formed the kind of bond drinkers sometimes will, sharing funny stories about our classmates, philosophizing on the transience of dreams, the fickleness of fate, the remoteness of love.

We talked for hours. It was the first time I had been able to be honest about how scared and confused I was about my life. Until then, my crash-and-burn in college had been like one of those dreams you have in which the teacher gives you a test you haven't studied for, or the final exam you slept through. Somehow, I kept expecting to wake up and find myself in front of a jury, with my beautiful wife waiting for me to finish my closing statement so we could go and pick out patio furniture. Instead, I spent my days sandblasting the charred remains of burned out buildings, coughing up stuff at the end of the day that looked like partially digested charcoal briquets. What would my beautiful wife say about that?

Stewart and I were like high school refugees. Most of my crowd were still in college, moving inexorably toward that patio furniture; most of his were married or in trouble, or both. We were left with each other, and began spending all our time together, going all kinds of places together virtually every weekend for the next two years. We shared enough adventures — and misadventures — to fill a book, and along the way we counseled each other through any number of crises.

Today, I am much less certain about the future than I was when I was 18. But just because I can't see, it doesn't mean I don't have one, and whether I have one or not, it's more important to live now than dream about patio furniture. Fifteen years ago, a close friend helped an ex-college boy figure that out. Beats anything I learned in pre-law.

AN EXPENSIVE RACCOON

I knew that my career as a high-stakes gambler would be short-lived when I lost 256 dollars trying to win a stuffed raccoon.

The carnival was in town, and I was trying to knock down three bowling pins with a softball tethered to the end of a stick. The barker seduced me by demonstrating how easy it was, pushing the ball out a couple of feet, then waiting for it to swoosh back and wipe out the pins. He could do it every time, without even looking. He had a tattoo of a buxom woman on his forearm, and when the ropy muscles in his arm flexed, the woman seemed to shiver with desire, bathed as she was there in the blue and green lights along the midway. Boy, did I want to gamble. There were women like that out there, wanting raccoons. All it cost was a quarter, and if you won, you not only got the raccoon—a very impressive creature any woman would love—you got your money back as well.

So, as a high-stakes gambler, I put down my quarter and took dead aim...and knocked down two pins, leaving the third upright, trembling as if wanting to fall, but afraid.

"Bet another quarter, son, and you'll get that raccoon for nothing," said the barker, and in handing me the ball he brought the tattoo-woman so close I could make out dimples and crevices. Someone had done some really meticulous work. "I'll give you back your original quarter as well as this spectacular raccoon!"

I held the ball and sized up the pins like Greg Maddux shaking off a sign for a curve. I was going to mow 'em down with my vaunted fastball. I was going to make that tattoo-woman dizzy with my heat. I was going home with that raccoon.

I knocked down one pin, leaving two standing tall and righteous as Promise Keepers. In those days, I might have made an excellent Promise Keeper—all I wanted to do was honor a submissive woman. It's all I really ever thought about.

"Better try again, son," said the barker. "Cost you fifty cents this time to get your money back. Just look at that raccoon. Any woman would love it!" The tattoo-woman writhed with anticipation.

By now, you, the reader, are beginning to get the drift. One dollar, two dollars, four dollars, eight dollars, sixteen dollars—a crowd forms around the panicky, beleaguered kid—thirty-two dollars, sixty-four dollars... The kid keeps waiting for Andy Taylor and Barney Fife to appear and close these crooks down, or for Mike Wallace to appear with a crew from "60 Minutes." Instead, the crowd simply gasps when the kid leaves yet another pin standing, having just spent sixty-four dollars in a desperate attempt to win...ah, forget that mangy raccoon, he needed that money back. It was the summer before college, and he'd been saving that money for a beach trip, where girls like the tattoo-woman were not only plentiful, but three-dimensional.

I told the barker I had only three dollars in my pocket, but I could go and get the other 125 dollars if he could only give me twenty minutes. Amazingly, he said he would be willing to wait for me. He felt sorry for me and said he wanted to see me win my money back (and get that raccoon!).

I proceeded to go withdraw what was left of my savings from the bank and return to the carnival, and the barker was nice enough to shoo away a couple of kids so I could at last knock over all three pins, salvage my beach trip and my self-respect, and win that handsome raccoon.

"C'mon, kid, you can do it this time," said the barker. As he handed me the ball, the tattoo-woman looked at me reproachfully, almost maternally.

Perhaps I could have, but I didn't. I knocked down two pins. I had lost 256 dollars. The barker's face twisted in agony.

"Kid, I don't want to take your money," he said, causing my heart to leap like a deer over the hood of an on-coming Volvo. "But I got no choice. House rules. Lookit, if you swear you won't tell anyone, I'll throw in this raccoon for nothing."

I took my raccoon and stood there watching other losers in love come and go, their hearts snatched by the lustrous tattoo-woman, their wallets by a barker with a heart of gold.

TRIPLE BYPASS

Tired, scared, anxious, and in need of a shave, I sat with my family in the intensive care unit at Baptist Hospital in Winston-Salem. Rather, I sat in the waiting room thumbing through months-old magazines, absorbing nothing I read, and as we all waited hungry for some morsel of news about my father's recovery from triple bypass heart surgery, it seemed to me at that moment that no place on this earth is as capricious as a hospital waiting room.

The patients were laid out in the next room side by side in an impossible web of tubes and lines running in and out of their bodies so that they resembled nothing so much as fallen puppets, perhaps waiting to be roused for the next show.

And some are roused. Several hours after my father's surgery was over, my brother and I stood by his side as his nurse explained the various readings on the spectacular computer above his head. The red numbers indicated his blood pressure, the green ones his heart rate, and so on. As we attempted to process all of this information while at the same time casting hopeful looks at our father's still and swollen face, the man in the next bed, not more than five feet away, began to come around. He made a noise first, then jostled about some, finally clutching a little at the tube which went down his throat in order to help his breathing.

His nurse seemed pleased that he was waking and spoke soothingly to him, informing him of his good condition, the terrific success of his surgery, and the need for him to relax now and let the machines do their work.

I had seen the whole thing, and I was moved by it all, every part, even his brief struggle with the breathing tube. He was back. He was going to live. That's how it seemed to me.

My brother asked our nurse whether our father would also be waking soon, and she assured us that he would, that the other man had just been brought in an hour earlier, and that our father was doing very well.

But he didn't wake an hour later. Or two hours later. Or even three. We saw some signs that he was beginning to breathe on his own, but he showed no signs of waking, even six hours after his surgery was over. The nurse, as well as a doctor, assured us that nothing was the matter; everything was still fine.

By the time the next visiting hour came around, at 8:15 p.m., word came that his eyes were open. Two by two, like animals boarding Noah's Ark, we went back to see him, and his eyes were open, and we tried not to seem too happy or too relieved because there was still much ahead of us and because there were still families in the waiting room who hadn't gotten the same assurances, the same signs, that we had gotten.

Over the course of two days, we got to know some of the other families a little, and we became very familiar with their names. Coontz, Doudy, Williams, Baker, Lattimore. And the Lindsays.

Mr. Lindsay was in with a blood clot on his brain. The doctors had operated on him the same day that my father had his heart surgery, and his family, like ours, had sweated it out. It was a risky surgery, the consequences uncertain.

But he made it through all right, and though no one went so far as to project much of anything right away, all his signs were stable through the night after the surgery and for most of the next day, which is supposed to be the critical period.

At about 2:30 p.m. on the day after both my father and Mr. Lindsay had their surgeries, I saw my father, who was now able to sit up and talk with us, though he was still in considerable pain and still hooked up to a network of tubes. But he was awake, and he was talking, and the relief I felt cannot be adequately described.

A little later, in the waiting room, Mrs. Lindsay came over and sat next to me. I would guess her age to be around 75, and she was flocked by two daughters, a son, two granddaughters, and another couple, friends of the family.

She asked me how our father was doing, and I told her he was getting along very well, and I asked her about Mr. Lindsay.

"Well," she said, "He's not too good. His signs are bad, and his organs are about shut down. He was doing fine this morning, and now his organs are shutting down. They said he wasn't going to make it. They said he'd be gone soon."

I was blank, dumb. I said I was sorry.

One of her daughters told me that they had lost a daughter in May. She was 39 and died of a heart attack.

"It was a massive heart attack," Mrs. Lindsay said. "They couldn't even operate. He never got over that. I ain't either."

Then she began to cry, but just barely, and other family members helped her up and just like that, they were out of the room and on their way back to look at Mr. Lindsay dying, just a bed or two away from my father.

Why, in her enormous, incomprehensible grief, had she asked about my father? Was she looking for some sign that hope was still alive in someone else that had gone out in her, or whether someone had robbed her of her parcel?

Did she need to know that someone, anyone, was going to make it out of there that day, or was she simply making "normal" waiting room conversation, too shocked to assimilate yet this sudden, final turn?

I don't have any answers for these questions. But I do remember the night before my dad was going into surgery, sitting with him in his room, nervously reading over a booklet on open heart surgery, watching Monday night football on TV, eating his lime sherbet, even answering "Jeopardy" questions, all of these banalities made precious by the fast approach of a new day.

That day came and went, and my father remains, either by caprice or by the grace of God or whatever good fortune may be. And for a time, for this time right now, all of life's banalities — picking up a napkin or pouring a glass of water — seem sweeter, very sweet.

That is the only answer I have for the moment, and for the moment that answer will do.

"I'M EATING AN APPLE"

My father, who is still recovering from triple-bypass heart surgery, called me up the other night just to check on how things were going. He sounded a little grumpy.

"What's going on?" I asked. "You seem a little out of sorts."

"I'm eating an apple," he said.

An apple. For many of you readers out there, eating an apple may not seem remarkable, certainly not something to call the immediate family about—"Hello, son, I've decided to eat an apple. I just thought you should know."

But you haven't met my father. If you had, you would understand how shattering such news actually is. After 55 years on this planet, the man has discovered fruit. Startling. In this post-operative world, he is like an astronaut hurtling through space, encountering things he's never dreamed of. Like exercise. And apples.

"I'm eating an apple." How surreal.

Apples were not part of my father's pre-operative world. For him, the four basic food groups consisted of Spam, biscuits and gravy, Coca Cola, and anything filled with crème. I had visions of him at Halloween, going into Food Lion and stocking up with enormous bags full of Snickers bars and candy corn (vegetable!), then turning off all the lights in his home and hunkering down in the bathtub in his wingtip shoes and brown slacks, eating all the candy as fast as he could before some little band of Frankensteins found him out.

The trick-or-treat police.

I remember how, after his first heart attack, he went on a radical health food kick, going so far as to order a Tab with his fried eggs, bacon, hash browns, and—yep—biscuits and gravy. On a plate like that one, who has room for wheat germ?

"I'm eating an apple." Yeah, dad, and I'm playing clarinet with a tone-deaf wolverine.

Still, if the idea of my father chomping on a Golden Delicious is enough to rattle the skull, what about the prospect of him in a sweat suit, sneakers and wrist bands, walking around a track, perhaps with a Sony Walkman, maybe keeping his pace matched to a Madonna tune? Why not? Things can't get much weirder.

I did actually see him exercise once. Well, sort of. What happened was that he had pulled in a ringer in a tennis doubles match against a couple of his unsuspecting buddies, who were so impressed with his athletic prowess that they were willing to bet a large sum of money on the match without even knowing the identity of his partner. For all they knew, he could have been teaming up with Jimmy Connors.

Of course, when the big day arrived, I had to be there. I thought of the irony as I sat in the parking lot at the tennis court, waiting on my father and his partner, the ringer, to arrive. I had become the parent, hoping my kid would do well. I wanted to play the match for him. Ah, bull nostrils. What I really wanted was to see him in terry cloth shorts and a head band. What I really wanted was to get just one look at his own special brand of the serve and volley.

When he did arrive, he was indeed decked out in standard tennis attire—a button down shirt, brown slacks, and wingtip shoes. He approached the court with a Marlboro in one hand and a Coke in the other.

"Where's your racket?" I said.

"I was hoping to borrow yours," he said.

He and his partner did go on to win the match and the bet, and I have come to believe that his "unusual" behavior at the court that day was psychological—a snickering opponent is a weakened opponent. He even made a few good shots, smashing errant lobs and poor second serves with authority.

I was so overwhelmed by this display that I bought him his own racket and an actual tennis outfit, which, as far as I know, is still packed in the same box with the ceramic frog ashtray I made him at 4-H camp in the fifth grade.

Perhaps, since he no longer has any use for the ashtray, he will rediscover his passion for tennis and with it his racket and outfit. Perhaps, in the not-too-distant future, I will get another phone call.

"I'm working on my backhand...By the way, do you know where I can find any pre-marinated tofu?"

A MAN IN UNIFORM

My friend Warren may be a candidate for the militia. What does it take to be a candidate? you ask. I'm not really sure, but I would guess it helps to believe in at least one significant governmental conspiracy theory above and beyond the one involving Kennedy's assassination. Another plus would be if you enjoyed dressing up in camouflage and playing around in the woods on weekends. If you are convinced that your inability to purchase a nuclear warhead at your local sporting goods store is a clear violation of your Second Amendment right to keep and bear arms, I'd say you're a shoo-in.

Warren and I both showed certain signs of militia aptitude in grade school. He enjoyed crawling around in the mud on his belly, firing his cap pistol at imaginary foes (United Nations' soldiers?) during recess, while I was content to deploy my G.I. Joe with The Kung Fu Grip in various tactical maneuvers in the classroom, such as hiding him under cushions so that when an unwitting girl sat down, her buttocks would be stabbed by his plastic bayonet.

Of course, there were many conspiracies. There was a conspiracy to keep us from getting all A's on our report cards, for example, and a conspiracy to prevent Peggy Ann Reeves from agreeing to be my valentine, even though I offered her a crisp new dollar bill to sweeten the deal.

There were conspiracies involving our allowances, curfews, and the amount of television we got to watch on week nights. There was a conspiracy to keep us off the football team and out of the Beta Club.

We didn't know enough then to blame it all on Nixon (we learned, though, we learned). In those days of innocence, our parents WERE the government, and, hell no, it was no democracy.

It was a conspiracy.

I lost interest in and track of my G.I. Joe. I think he may have left the country with Action Barbie. It's just as well. By the time I had finished putting him through all those tactical maneuvers involving the puncturing of girls' buttocks, he was down to one leg and no arms, his legendary Kung Fu Grip lost in battle.

I also lost interest in conspiracy theories. This is not to suggest that I don't still harbor serious suspicions about what goes on in Washington; it's just that I don't believe Jesse Helms and Ted Kennedy are plotting with United Nations operatives to bust down my door and take my guns, break my pencils, and shave my dogs or whatever.

Warren, on the other hand, is not quite prepared to relinquish his own conspiracy theories. For instance, he believes that there is a conspiracy among dentists to ruin our teeth. He believes that when dentists give us the fluoride treatment or brush our teeth with that gritty, toothpaste-like substance, they are actually sabotaging our teeth with a potent, enamel-destroying concoction (sort of a Hershey's Bar, to the 10th power) designed to cause cavities within a six-month period.

"Think about it," he said. "Are dentists going to put themselves out of business by preventing cavities? I don't think so."

He thinks that flossing is a hoax as well.

"Have you ever seen anyone from the United Nations flossing? I rest my case."

Warren also believes that conspiracies reach into the sports world. He maintains that the government is responsible for boxer Mike Tyson's woes (Warren lost a hundred bucks in the Buster Douglas fight) and last year's baseball strike, which he contends was the only way to keep the Cleveland Indians (his favorite team) out of the World Series.

He blames his receding hairline on the government, as well as his poor singing voice and that hissing noise his car makes.

These are the sort of "special" insights that make Warren an ideal candidate for the militia, though now that he's out of shape and rather dangerously near-sighted, I do worry about him taking part in those weekend drills.

Maybe he can answer phones, send out fliers, or make coffee for the other guys. One wonders, is there room for a receptionist in this man's army?

THE NATURE BOY!

Do you remember the day you discovered that your hero had feet of clay? My friend Warren remembers. For him, it happened when the "Nature Boy" Ric Flair was arrested for driving while intoxicated. Rather, a 20-year-old girl was arrested for the actual driving; Flair was arrested since it was his car and he had allowed the girl, who is not old enough to drink, to drive it.

Warren and I have been following the exploits of the "Nature Boy" since we were in the third grade. In case you don't know, Flair is a professional wrestler who burst upon the scene in the early 1970s as the purported younger cousin of the Minnesota Wrecking Crew, Gene and Ole Anderson, the greatest tag team the sport has ever known.

At this point I think it is only fair to warn those readers who may be contemplating a letter complaining how professional wrestling is not a sport that, if you do send one, you may expect Warren to hunt you down and put you in the dreaded Chicken Wing hold, or perhaps the Figure Four, Flair's trademark submission maneuver. It would be a kind of homage to the master, who has been embarrassed by what Warren assures me are trumped-up charges.

You see, Warren idolizes Flair, who is regarded by some as "the dirtiest player in the game" and is regarded by himself as a "high flyin', jet ridin', kiss stealin', wheelin' dealin', stylin' and profilin' son of a gun. Woooo!"

Flair says "Woooo" a lot, which is one of the qualities Warren particularly admires. He respects a confident man. In fact, Warren says "Woooo" a lot himself, though admittedly not to the same effect. Somehow, outside the realm of the professional wrestling arena, "Woooo" just fails to resonate: "Honey, I'm going to the store. Woooo! We're out of Vienna sausages. Woooo!"

Or maybe it's just that Flair does it with such aplomb. In any case, Warren has been imitating his idol since grade school, when he got a plain white tee shirt printed with the words "Nature Boy" on the front and wore it to school every day for three weeks, until the assistant principal called his mother and asked if there was some problem. (Warren had been sneaking the shirt to school in his duffel bag and changing on the bus.)

The words "Nature Boy" were, for some, enigmatic. The English teacher, for example, thought Warren might be a budding Thoreau even though he had failed, thus far, to grasp the distinction between nouns and verbs. Might've been one of those Einstein deals—can't tie his shoes because he's preoccupied figuring out the theory of relativity.

Another teacher tried to get Warren signed up for scouts, interpreting his shirt as a sign that he had a deep love for the outdoors and needed to spend all his spare time camping. Amazingly, few of the teachers had gotten wind of the heroics of one Ric Flair, so they were quite understandably disappointed when Warren spurned all of their well-intentioned advances, opting instead for putting first graders in the sleeper hold and challenging stray dogs to cage matches in his spare time.

Over the course of the last 20 years, Warren says that he has seen Flair wrestle in person on 26 occasions. He has attempted to correspond—unsuccessfully—with the "Nature Boy" on various occasions through the years, though he did receive an 8 X 10 glossy with Flair's autograph a few years ago. And though it is clear that Flair has lost a step or two and his once bulging body now sags in a place or two, Warren is adamant that the "Nature Boy" is as good a wrestler as he's ever been, compensating for the decrease in his physical prowess with the experience and guile that only a grizzled veteran can boast of. Wooooo!

That is why the news of his arrest was especially troubling for Warren. Why would Flair do it? Would he be suspended? Stripped of his championship belt? (Flair has been world wrestling champion 12 times—take that, Mike Tyson!)

Warren suspects foul play.

"It was a set-up, man. Probably Hulk Hogan and the Macho Man. They're all jealous of Flair, and they always have been. I'll bet it wasn't even a real cop. I'll bet it wasn't even a real reporter. If he loses the belt, those guys are going to pay dearly. He'll run 'em out of town."

Warren needn't have worried. On the night after the news broke, Flair appeared on television with his belt in tow, flanked on either side by the mysterious "Woman" and "Miss Elizabeth," ex-wife of the Macho Man, who abandoned her husband and helped Flair defeat him for the championship belt (Flair knocked him out with one of her high heels), thus joining the "Nature Boy" on his continuing reign of terror.

Clearly, it will take more than a few Heinekens, an underage girl, and a fake cop to bring down the "Nature Boy." Wooooo!

DEAR CINDY

My friend Warren thinks he may have a shot at Cindy Crawford. Yes, that Cindy Crawford, the one who is a famous model, the one who recently separated from her husband Richard Gere, the actor and Buddhist, who was so shaken by the prospect of his impending divorce that he sought solace in Tibet, hanging out with the Dalai Lama and a redheaded model.

Warren thinks his time has come. Recently, he was watching Cindy on her television show, MTV's "House of Style," and he is sure he sensed in her doe eyes a need for comfort, a desire for stability, a shattering cry for a radical change in her circumstances.

"She doesn't realize how unhappy she is," Warren said. "She doesn't know what she needs."

What type of comfort would Cindy Crawford need to assuage her pain? Fake brick wallpaper? Spaghetti-Os every night? A strobe light and incense? Such are the comforts of Warren's lifestyle.

"You're going to provide stability for Cindy Crawford?" I asked.

"Well, let's put it this way. I'm not going to run off to Tibet."

"Warren, you couldn't afford a weekend in Raleigh."

"That's the point, man. Cindy's sick of the glamor. She doesn't care about money. Can't you see that? She wants something else now, something real. Richard Gere is an actor. He acts. She never knew if he really cared about her or if it was just another scene from *An Officer and a Gentleman*. You can't live that way, man."

"So, how are you going to let her know that you're the solution to all her problems?"

"I sent her a valentine. I wrote stuff on it. I slipped in a snapshot of myself."

"Uh-oh."

"I'm telling you, man. Appearances aren't Cindy's game anymore. She's had it up to here with plastic surgeons and tummy tucks and grapefruit diets. All she needs is to spend a nice Friday evening watching Kung Fu movies with a pint of Ben and Jerry's ice cream."

"And you?"

"I'm the missing ingredient, man."

"And you figure the valentine ought to show her the light?"

I tried to picture it. Cindy Crawford, cover girl, resigning from her show, leaving the business, moving to a small town in North Carolina, moving into Warren's little studio apartment above the hardware store, getting her a key made downstairs, warming up a can of pork and beans on the hot plate, telling Warren why things went sour with Richard, selecting ice cream on Friday afternoons at Bi-Lo, cultivating the life of the mind.

She'd need a job. Maybe she could pursue her career, after all, hawking cars on the local cable channel, maybe coaxing lawsuits out of people who didn't realize they were injured for disreputable lawyers.

"Hi, I'm Cindy Crawford. Have you been injured in an accident? Slipped on a wet floor? Been burned by hot chocolate? Seen a hair in your soup? Then you may be entitled to damages. We here at the law firm of (expletive deleted) want to help soothe your pain by procuring a tidy settlement..."

Warren, the hopeless romantic, told her in the valentine that she wouldn't have to work, but might want to so that they could afford to move into another apartment, perhaps one with a real stove, one without the myriad sensory delights of hardware below.

"What if she doesn't call or write back?" I asked him.

"She will, she will," he said. "And if she doesn't, I sent another valentine to Heather Locklear. I saw her the other night on Barbara Walters, and, boy, did she seem miserable."

When it comes to the whirlwind world of celebrity courtships, I guess it's important to keep your options open.

DEATH BY GARLIC

My friend Warren has always been a hypochondriac. Years ago, when I was too young to drive, Warren, who was a few years older, used to let me and a couple of other guys my age drive his burgundy Nova up and down the back roads until we got bored. Then we'd get some cheap, screwtop wine and head to the drycleaners in town, where we'd drink and watch cars go by until two or three o'clock in the morning.

The drycleaners was closed, of course, but Warren played tennis with the owner, an older guy named Barney, who had entrusted him with a key to the place. I couldn't imagine the circumstances in which Warren would ever need or ask for a key to a drycleaners, but what did it matter — it was a haven for us to go and do as we pleased, right under the cops' noses, and we took mighty advantage of it for quite some time, until Barney finally grew tired of shampooing the carpet every Sunday evening to alleviate the not-too-fetching fragrance of peach wine and vomit, with just a hint of pepperoni.

"The customers don't want to smell that stuff when they come to get their shirts cleaned," Barney would say.

Even though we kept breaking promises not to foul up his drycleaners, I guess Barney kept cutting us some slack because he was convinced Warren was dying of some rare, untreatable disease. Warren, of course, was also convinced.

"I'm not going to make it until Valentine's Day," he would say. "My heartbeat is twice what it should be, I haven't eaten anything but celery and shredded wheat for three weeks, and my pancreas still feels inflamed. Of course, these incompetent backwoods doctors can't find anything, but if I could afford to go to Duke, I'm sure they would conclude that the condition I suffer from cannot be cured."

I have known Warren for more than twenty years now, and he has been on the brink of death since I met him. He has been to every doctor in the area, talked to pharmacists, read medical journals, and tried every herb, medicine, and diet imaginable. Still, the poor man suffers. One of the interesting things about going home to visit is getting the latest update on Warren's condition. His maladies are never ordinary.

"I think my fingernails are going to fall off," he said a couple of years ago. "I've been feeling a lot of pain in the tips of my fingers, like someone is sticking needles underneath my nails. I've been taking a lot of zinc, and, for the last four days, I haven't eaten anything but bananas and ginger ale, but it's not getting any better. There's no way I'm going to live until Halloween."

Is it any wonder, then, that I was looking forward to seeing Warren last week while I was home for Christmas? I had had a touch of the flu recently, but no matter how poorly I might be feeling, I knew one thing for certain: Warren would be feeling much worse. Sure enough, when I phoned him on Christmas Eve to see if he wanted to go see "Titanic," a movie I thought he could relate to quite well, Warren sounded typically weak and forlorn.

"Well, I guess we could go," he said. "If you won't drive over 40 miles per hour. I've changed medications, and my heart is racing like a dog around a track after a rabbit. I didn't sleep two hours last night."

When I arrived at his house, Warren came out and opened the car door on the passenger side. Immediately, I was almost physically knocked over by a thunderous wave of garlic. Oh no, I thought, not this. Was I going to have to spend the next five or six hours with a 140-pound clove of garlic?

When he got in and shut the door, Warren pretended nothing was wrong, even though I drove with my nose pressed as close to the crack in my window as I could manage and still operate the vehicle.

"If I don't do something about my blood count, I might as well jump off a bridge," he said. "My only hope is raw garlic..."

"Warren, if we don't do something about that smell, I'm going to drive off the bridge," I said. "I'm going to hose you down with some air freshener, and if you've got any garlic on you, you'd better pitch it out."

"Fine, why don't you just shoot me while you're at it?"

Might as well, since the poor fellow clearly has no chance of making it to Easter anyway. He'd probably smell better soaked in formaldehyde.

THE BAD ATTITUDE CLUB

My brother is thinking of becoming a high school principal. He currently teaches English at the same high school he, my sister, and I all attended, and, for me, it is a singularly bizarre experience when I'm visiting my hometown and drop by to see him at the school. Here is my little brother, all grown up, teaching and coaching at my old high school, and someday soon he may well be the principal. Bizarre? How about surreal.

Maybe this will strike you as strange, but when I step inside the doors of my old high school, I am suddenly transported back to 1978, when I was a sophomore struggling to make the basketball team and stay awake in biology class. My friends and I spent our lunch period in the parking lot inside my old, wrecked Buick Electra, jury-rigging the eight-track tape player with a matchbook so we could jam out to Black Sabbath and smoke unfiltered cigarettes while our college prep peers choked down chuckwagon sandwiches inside.

Though I'm a grown man now, when I'm there I am suddenly the same nervous, skinny, stubbornly rebellious kid I was then, more worried about a pimple forming on my forehead than passing social studies.

As you may have inferred from these details, my career as a high school student was less than stellar. I despised the school mightily, all my teenage angst coiled up inside me and ready to spring like a bear trap. I cultivated indifference, made a show of it, rarely bothering to make it to class. When my beloved basketball went sour, I co-founded something called the "Bad Attitude Club." We even had T-shirts made in school colors and wore them to school every Friday. Predictably, our new "club" was not met with much enthusiasm by the faculty, and, just as predictably, we couldn't have cared less and didn't hesitate to let anyone within hearing range know it.

Like most kids who court disaster, I eventually found it. My grades were terrible, I stayed in trouble constantly, and I couldn't wait to graduate and go on to college, which had become for me the Emerald City, where I would at last get a life.

Then I got arrested. It had been a long standing custom for seniors to paint the water tower during the week of graduation — you know, "Class of '80," stuff like that. Nobody in authority really seemed to care; it was expected, and it was excused. For me, there as just one problem. I was deathly afraid of heights. Scaling any sort of tower was unthinkable. And there was another problem. We were the "Bad Attitude Club," which meant we were bad. We couldn't abide defacing something that had already been stamped with the school's seal of approval. What kind of weak vandalism was that? We decided to go for something bigger, something that would be a gesture, something that would be symbolic. We decided to paint the activity bus.

So, late one night, we painted "Class of '80" and "B.A.C." in huge, gaudy orange letters all over the bus. It was masterful. It was bold. It was incredibly, incredibly stupid.

The next day was a school day, and we were practicing for graduation, arranging the lineup and learning our cues and so on. Then the police arrived. They set up shop in the principal's office and, in short order, began summoning suspects for questioning. Of course, I was one of the first to be called.

It was really pretty grand. I felt a little nauseous, but I also felt a little like James Cagney. I wasn't going to crack, and I certainly wasn't going to turn state's evidence against my friends, come what may. I was led into the room by a muscular officer with red, neatly cropped hair and severe eyes, and another, smaller, slightly pudgy officer, who matter-of-factly read me my Miranda rights. As soon as he was finished, the other officer told me that one of my fellow Bad Attitude Club members had ratted us out and that I might as well come clean. I thought it might be entrapment, but since I hadn't paid attention in social studies, I couldn't be sure.

So I lawyered up. I told them I had nothing to say outside the presence of my attorney. Then I looked at my shoes, which I hadn't really noticed since they had been covered by my graduation gown until I sat down. I was wearing a pair of wretched blue suede Adidas sneakers, only now they were wretched blue suede Adidas sneakers with enormous, obnoxious orange splotches on them. Paint. In legal parlance, I believe this is called "strong circumstantial evidence."

The gig was up, and I knew it. Ultimately, we were allowed to graduate, though some strongly objected, and we were given many hours of community service by a very generous judge who had, thankfully, never heard of the Bad Attitude Club.

Now, when I drop by the school to see my brother, I can't escape the feeling that I'm somehow being watched, that I'm up to something, that I'm skipping biology class, that I've got paint on my shoes. I know that I have gone on to achieve some measure of success, but when I'm in that school I'm as shaky as Kato Kaelin at a Quiz Bowl.

If my brother ever becomes principal, I guess I'll still go by and see him in the principal's office. But I may wind up needing therapy to get through it.

CHILD STAR

It was a sweltering summer Saturday night. Hundreds of cars crawled the street surrounding my old elementary school auditorium, looking for parking spaces like old couples on the beach looking for sand dollars. Bats sliced the lamplight, making crazy dives into darkness.

Everyone in town, it seemed, was here for my niece's dance recital. Well, all right, there were other children, too, but for each member of the audience, the spotlight lingered on one child especially. For my family, it was Katelyn, six-year-old prodigy of the stage, our fairy princess in gilded slippers.

There were three generations of us sitting there — me, my mother, my grandmother, and my sister, mother of the star performer. The fourth generation would soon take center stage. Well, all right, maybe not center stage, but somewhere on the stage, conspicuous as a leopard among tabby cats.

We fanned ourselves with our programs, pointed out familiar children in leotards and sequins, and bided our time. Katelyn was to appear in no fewer than three dances.

As I sat there, I reflected on how lucky she was to be born of such fine performing stock. My sister, at about the same age as Katelyn, had left an audience in that very same auditorium in stunned silence years ago when, moments after the curtain was raised on her debut as a stage performer, she bolted from the stage in tears rather than mime the words to "I'm a little tea pot, short and stout, Here is my handle, here is my spout."

I am sorry to report that on the way off stage, my sister tripped in her cumbersome tea kettle costume, breaking her spout in the process, which caused her to cry even more loudly. Alas, there was no encore.

Though I do not wish to boast, I must nevertheless confess that my career on the stage was no less distinguished than my sister's. I once played a shepherd in our church's Christmas play, which was a juicy part, considering that the role of the baby Jesus was played by a forty-watt light bulb. I even had a line.

"Hark!" I said.

I was so fond of this line and my command of it that I repeated it every so often during the play, even though I was supposed to deliver it just once. When I uttered it at inappropriate moments, I caught Mary and Joseph giving me mean looks.

Clearly, with such rich Thespian blood coursing through her veins, Katelyn had a lot to live up to.

At last, she appeared in her fairy costume, second from the left in a row of fairies all waving magic wands, ostensibly to the beat of some song I can't quite remember. She was, of course, radiant.

After some discussion amongst the family, we agreed that the performance was avant-garde, since in the previous performances all the dancers had been in perfect matched precision, while in this one it appeared that no two fairies were doing even approximately the same thing.

"How daring!" I said. "How cutting edge!"

At one juncture, Katelyn seemed to come perilously close to puncturing the eye of another fairy with her wayward wand, but I thought it might be part of the performance, perhaps a threat of tragedy thrown in for dramatic impact. Bold! Bravo!

The other two performances were no less spellbinding, no less complexly choreographed, no less pure art.

After the recital, we all greeted our star with gushing reviews of her performance, though I believe she was more interested in getting some french fries than having these accolades heaped upon her. She waved her wand and we were off, transported from our teakettle dreams to the magical land of the Whopper.

"BIRTHPLACE OF DEL REEVES"

I was on vacation during the past week in my hometown of Sparta, NC, birthplace of the country music semi-superstar Del Reeves, who sang the semi-smash hit "Girl on the Billboard" and was something of a Nashville luminary some 20-25 years back. At the city limits, there is a sign that reads, "Welcome to Sparta, home of Del Reeves." My grandmother lives next door to Del's brother, Homer. Every so often, Homer's coon dogs get loose and roam around the neighborhood, pausing every few yards to mark the next tree or bush with that special signature for which dogs are famous.

I never knew Del, who was already gone to Nashville before I was born, but I've known Homer all my life. I spent a lot of time during my childhood at my grandmother's house, and I became good friends with Homer's grandson, Greg, who was about two years younger than I. We played whiffle ball in the yard, using a bush, a small tree, and the corner of a flowerbed as bases. If you hit it to the creek, it was an automatic home run. He pretended he was Reggie Jackson or Johnny Bench, and I was Don Sutton or Phil Niekro. We played for hours, then spent the balance of those long summer days tormenting our younger siblings with practical jokes, outrageous lies, and interminable teasing. Greg's sister Laurinda was a six-year-old hellion who could hold her own even in the face of our most fiendish plots against her; she was a tremendously skilled "fake crier," able to sob hysterically on cue and bring their mother Laurene to the porch with her hands planted on her hips. Sometimes, if she was inspired sufficiently, Laurinda would allege that Greg had hit her, when in fact he might have done nothing more injurious than chase her around the yard brandishing a baby black snake in a Mason jar, or maybe just a simple dried dog turd.

It didn't matter. The verdict was always the same. Laurene instructed Greg to go and cut a hickory switch to be whipped with. If the switch was not satisfactory, Laurene herself would go and cut it, and the whipping would be twice as bad. From my detached vantage point, this form of punishment struck me as particularly sadistic, and therefore marvelous. Here was a direct descendant of Del Reeves about to get his bare legs striped with red welts by a hickory switch of his own choosing, and I would get to see the entire thing. My own mother, bless her, lacked the temperament for such medieval corrective actions, preferring the "wait-til-your-dad-gets-home" method of discipline.

Not Laurene. She was the very epitome of hands-on. Her arm and that switch were just a blur, like a hummingbird's wings, and she pivoted around in circles, holding Greg with one arm while blistering his legs with the other. It was like something pure, and Greg shrieked so loudly with cries of repentance that Homer would be roused from his afternoon nap and come to stand in the shade of his enormous maple tree and watch the proceedings with a grim face.

A few years later, when I finally was old enough to drive, I'd sometimes find myself trapped behind Homer on the winding road that led to town. There was no place to pass, and Homer has always been famous for never exceeding 25 miles per hour in his ancient white Ford pickup. On the bumper, there was a decal which read, fittingly, "I May Be Slow, But I'm Ahead of You." In the pickup bed, the coon dogs, who always liked to ride into town, danced around like Fred Astaire and Ginger Rogers.

Now, all these years later, Greg has his own business in Winston-Salem, Laurinda is happily married with kids of her own, Del still sings the same songs that made him famous, and Homer still has his coon dogs. Saturday night, as I was visiting my grandmother, I happened to look out the window just in time to see the brown one marking his territory on my left front tire.

The next morning, my last day in Sparta for a few more months, I got behind Homer on my way to town. The coon dogs' heads bobbed like apples in a barrel at the Halloween carnival. Fifteen miles per hour. He may be slow, but he's still ahead of me.

Part III: Great Insights and Other Delights

A MAP OF WAX CITIES

What's it been, now, ten years since I've seen her? It's not as if I haven't kept up. A few years ago, I showed up out of nowhere at her parents' house. It had been four or five years since we split up, and they were shocked when I called from a nearby pay phone. All that time had gone by, and she was married to a guy they didn't much like, and I was married then, too. Within half an hour, I was sitting at their kitchen table while her mom piled me with heaping platefuls of fried squash, and her dad told me how rotten things had been lately at Chatham's, the trucking company he drove for.

I ate fried squash and drank iced tea, and we sat and looked at each other, and what we were all thinking was that it could have turned out this way, but didn't, and that I would probably never see either one of them again because, in life, when you lose the girl you lose the family, too, and that's just the way it goes, no matter how you feel. We had lost each other. I told them that I had loved them as I did my own family, and her father cried, and her mom looked out the window between slants in the Venetian blind and said, "Ooh, law...ooh, law."

I think of her sometimes when it snows. I met her during winter, and one night, in the midst of a snowstorm, she took off all her clothes and ran around her apartment building stark naked in the driving snow. I thought, here's someone I could love. Hope she doesn't fall. Later, covered in an old quilt her grandmother made, we watched how the colored Christmas lights, strung along the gutters, reflected patterns on the snow, and the very ground itself seemed something made just for us.

Inside, the room was dark except for the feeble light of two candles burning on either side of us. She took one, a big round one, and poured a pool of aqua-colored wax on my arm while I tried not to flinch. Then, dipping a finger, she traced lines from my elbow to the back of my hand, pausing sometimes to leave a dollop no larger than a dime. "Here's a town," she said. "And here's one." Thus, I became a map of wax cities, and my fingers, extended, were like highways that might have lead anywhere. For the first time in my life, I was exactly where I wanted to be. All my life, I had been plagued by the vague notion that the life I wanted was going on somewhere else without me. Suddenly, that was all gone. I took the candle from her and held it to her eyes, which were sometimes gray and sometimes hazel.

"We're going to be snowed in tomorrow," she said.

A few months later, we got engaged in a disco. The Gap Band's "You Dropped the Bomb on Me" blared, and she was dancing with one of my friends. I had been working out and had my shirtsleeves rolled to my armpits, concocting reasons to flex my arms so the veins in my biceps would pop out. We danced a slow one under the big, glittering disco ball, and when I dipped my head down to smell the papaya-scented shampoo in her hair, I told her that I always wanted it to be this way, that I would never leave her, that I would die if I couldn't have her forever, and that I would, with my bulging biceps, kill anyone who stood between us and our future together. And I believed every word that I said.

Forever lasted about two years. We didn't get married. I didn't kill anyone. I went back to college, and she stayed behind. I'd come home to see her on weekends, but things began to change, and neither one us could do one thing about it. Finally, the incongruity between what we had wanted and what we actually had became too great for either of us, and she broke off the engagement. A couple of weeks later, I panicked and called her in a desperate effort to breathe life into the relationship, but I got the recording we all dread: "This number is no longer in use."

I haven't seen or spoken to her since. Ten years. Still, sometimes, late at night, when the past settles over me like mist on a lake, I will drip candle wax onto my arm in little drops, and I imagine distant cities, places I will never travel, lives I will never know, and I try to remember that my life is going on right here with me now. Even so, I catch myself wondering if her eyes still burn from gray to hazel in the glow of candlelight on a winter's night.

YOU GOTTA KNOW WHEN TO FOLD 'EM

I had never been to the Cherokee casino or any casino until my friend, Stewart, and his fiancee, Tammy, came down for a visit a couple of months ago and dragged me over there. Stewart has about as much interest in gambling as I do—none, unless you count love, on which we've both bet and lost. As far as I'm concerned, love is a bad pony. You'd probably be better off betting on the Packers, but who wants to sleep with them?

In any event, I had very little interest in going to the casino, even when I heard Pat Benatar would be playing there soon and maybe even three of the Four Tops (slogan: 75 percent original Tops!). Somehow, the prospect of blowing a hundred bucks on a fruity little arcade game while washed-up musicians played warmed-over sets to bankrupt tourists didn't exactly sound like my idea of a good time. Plus, I had read all about the dangers of gambling addiction and the influx of organized crime that gambling was sure to bring to the reservation. I pictured myself pawning the tires off my car in a desperate attempt to get three plums to line up, then getting gunned down by somebody in the Gambino family because I spilled Diet Pepsi on the shoes of some "made guy" playing the slot machine next to me.

No, I didn't really want to go. But Tammy did. She's quite a gambler, we discovered, having been to Vegas on a number of occasions and having developed strategies to improve her odds at a number of different games. In this respect, she differs from my father, who is the only other serious gambler I've ever known. As you're reading this, chances are 50-50 that he's in the middle of a poker game somewhere, replete with a fistful of crumpled, well-traveled bills in the middle of some rickety table surrounded by a bunch of equally rickety men, all sporting cigarettes and uneven sideburns.

My father is renowned in my hometown of Sparta, NC, as an excellent gambler, and though he prefers cards, he will bet on anything, including sports, politics, the weather, you name it. You think there's a cold front moving in? He's got twenty bucks that says there isn't. If two birds are sitting on a wire, he'll bet you ten dollars on which one will fly away first and beat you nine out of ten tries. Tammy relies on strategy to beat the game; my dad relies on instinct. And they both rely on nerve and a certain devil-may-care philosophy that, as far as I can tell, is essential among the hardcore gambling set.

For example, a veteran gambler's expression never changes one iota whether she is winning or losing. Once we got inside the casino, it took Tammy approximately 45 seconds to get herself ensconced in a blackjack game in which the minimum bet was five dollars. All the players wore identical faces: blank. Stewart and I decided to take a look around the place, leaving the suddenly blank-faced Tammy to her own devices while we surveyed the rows and rows of brightly colored, flashing machines.

Just an arcade for adults hoping to strike it rich, I thought, the same poor souls who subscribe to *Redbook* and *Field and Stream* in the eternal hope that Ed McMahon will appear at their door one day with a check the size of a tablecloth, made out to them in letters large enough for the whole world to read and admire. Everywhere I looked, people were lined up, pouring their silver money into these machines. I thought, if the Indians had had casinos when we came over on the Mayflower, we'd be the ones on the reservations now. Can't you just see the pilgrims huddled around the craps table, having lost everything, trying to win back just one oar off the boat to paddle home with?

As far as all the controversy is concerned, if people want to go to Cherokee and blow their money on gambling, so what? I always get very nervous when men in blue suits want to pass laws to protect us from ourselves. If I want to ride my motorcycle without a helmet, rent an adult movie, smoke unfiltered cigarettes for forty consecutive hours, or spend next month's rent at the blackjack table, just get out of my way. The freedom to choose does not always guarantee smart choices, as the many re-elections of Jesse Helms makes clear. Still, this is America, and people should have the right to make choices by their own lights, without government interference.

What percentage of the Four Tops agrees with this position remains unclear. And, for what it's worth, Tammy won $250 at the blackjack table, never once changing expression.

I LOVE YOU, YOU BEAST

I am in an abusive relationship with my weatherman.

He lies to me, tells me things I want to hear, then breaks all his promises. He has a trustworthy face and an expensive haircut and a pleasant golly-by-gosh demeanor, the very sort of fellow you'd like to see your sister hook up with.

Do not be fooled.

He'll dazzle you with fantastic graphics and extravagant maps, in front of which he moves around like some meteorological god, omniscient and generous. He woos you with impressive techno-weatherspeak, explaining the vagaries of high pressure systems and barometric something-or-others. He lets you look at his Doppler radar, its long, loving arm sweeping over your town like a giant windshield wiper, revealing cloud cover or clear skies just for you.

He implies a future together with seductive whispers of a five-day forecast. Oh, there may be rough days ahead, but he'll be right there with you come rain or shine. Just trust him.

I do, every time, and that's why I found myself trapped last Monday on I-40 east of Canton in a partly cloudy, light rain day disguised as a mini-blizzard. I had been on my way to Sparta to see family and friends and prepare for Christmas. My car was packed with gifts, and clothes, and various cassette tapes, and I was the very picture of confidence and good will as I approached Asheville around 9:30 a.m. Sure, there was a little flurry blowing around, but what did I care? I was armed with a forecast, the words of which were emblazoned in my mind like a lover's first poem: light rain, forty-one degrees.

Light rain, forty-one degrees.

Even as the flakes grew bigger — much bigger, pieces of some enormous frozen puzzle — and frantic faces pressed by in car window after car window, I felt peace in my heart as I recalled the assuring words of my weatherman, Gary Guessagin: *Light rain, forty-one degrees.*

As the "light rain" grew heavier and the road whiter, I elected to pull over and call someone in Sparta, a small town nestled way up in the Blue Ridge Mountains. I knew the weather here was a freak and would soon pass (*light rain, forty-one degrees* — a mantra now), but I was concerned that the weather there might be really treacherous.

I got through and was informed that traveling conditions were indeed poor, and that I had better postpone my arrival for a day or two. A little disappointed, I turned my car around and headed back to Waynesville. By now, the roads were basically white but for the tracks made by the traffic, which still seemed to be moving along rather briskly. Perhaps other drivers had heard the forecast after all, and knew that highways just do not get very slippery when the temperature is *forty-one degrees.*

In any case, we moved along cautiously, but at a goodly rate. Until we were about five miles east of Canton, that is. At this point, the roads were completely and utterly white, there were no discernible tracks, and traffic moved along at what might charitably be called a donkey-like pace.

The miles crawled by ominously like shadows outside a child's bedroom window in the dark, and with each passing mile there were more and more motorists stranded on the side of the road. Some stood by mangled fenders, others appeared dazed, like students who stayed up all night studying for the wrong exam.

I strangled the steering wheel with both hands, reminded myself to breathe periodically, and struggled along yard by yard in second gear, hovering around 15-20 miles per hour. I uttered oaths against the weatherman — no, I wouldn't take him back this time — then reproached myself both for my hostility and foul mouth. If only I could make it back, I'd live a virtuous life from that point forward. No more gluttony, or envy, or pride, or gossip. No more leaving the dishes until the next day, or underwear on the floor, or letters unanswered and phone calls unreturned.

I imagined all the features of my future exemplary life as I crept along the last four miles home, and I had plenty of time to do it since traffic now moved along like ketchup in that old commercial: anticipation, it's making me wait.

At last, I pulled into the driveway at my house and promptly collapsed, dizzy with relief and gratefulness. I thought ruefully of the weatherman. I felt duped, humiliated, and disillusioned, like some love struck dweeb waiting by the window for a date that's never coming, never was, and never will.

I thought of the weatherman as Lucy and myself as Charlie Brown, trying to kick the football. Each time, Lucy pulls it away at the last minute, and I am left flat on my back, looking up at nothing but *light rain, forty-one degrees.*

When I went inside and turned on the TV to check the news, there he was. Gary Guessagin. Looking sheepish, apologetic, humbled, even pleading. Scoundrel, I thought, vermin. Sorry sack of...there goes my exemplary life.

But he looked right at me and explained how it wasn't his fault, this piling snow. He showed me a marvelously fancy map of the United States, and he pointed to some arrows pointing upward from the Gulf of Mexico, and he swore that nobody could've predicted what had happened.

He promised to do better next time. He looked right into my eyes and said that.

I went to make a bowl of soup, and got back in time to catch the five-day forecast.

One more chance, one more chance, one more chance.

WAKING UP IN A CORNFIELD

Between the three of us, we had consumed four or five bottles of Boones Farm Tickled Pink the night before, and now we were beginning to wake — painfully, remorsefully, reluctantly — in the middle of some poor farmer's thriving cornfield. Where had we been headed? Hard to say, but now we were planted here among the other vegetables, with Fleetwood Mac groaning along at half speed on Loom's eight track tape player. Apparently, the tape had been playing all night and the car's battery was almost dead. I found myself caught in that unenviable gray area between wanting to vomit and wanting not to vomit, my exploding headache aggravated no doubt by the door lock knob that had been jammed into my temple for the past three or four hours. A vengeful rooster heralded the atrocious dawn.

Having battled off nausea, I took a quick inventory of my fellows. There was Loom in the front seat, his body twisted into an impossible position, arms and legs at odds with his torso. Where was Scott? In time, I ascertained that he was not in the car. With great effort, I managed to open the car door and stumble out. I must have looked like a newborn colt attempting to steady himself on untried legs. I found Scott just a few feet away, stretched out among fallen cornstalks. He had an abrasion over his right eye that he would be hard-pressed to explain to his parents later on; it was, to be sure, a hazy recollection, but I seemed to remember we had had a corn fight at some stage in the night's revelry, and it was conceivable that the wound was produced by a flying ear of corn. In any case, it was left to me to finish the rooster's work and bring my buddies to so we could put our throbbing heads together and find a way to jump-start a rusting Chevy Nova at 6:30 a.m. on a Sunday morning. In the middle of a cornfield. Eight miles from town. Fleetwood Mac sang, in groggy, quarter speed, "Don't stop thinking about tomorrow." A new wave of nausea threatened the ruined shores of my skull.

I was fifteen years old at the time, a high school sophomore and a binge drinker. I had drunk my first beer at the age of 12 at my friend Mark's new house. His mother had just remarried the wealthiest man in town, and they were off to Barbados, leaving the Jacuzzi and the rest of the mansion to a couple of 12-year-old boys and a 20-year-old babysitter whose man problems led her to make an ill-advised pact with us: If we would behave, we could stay up as late as we wanted as long as we didn't tell that she had left us there alone to go check up on her boyfriend's cheating heart and wandering eye. Deal, we said, waiting no more than fifteen minutes after she left to grab a couple of baby Millers out of the well-stocked fridge and head to the Jacuzzi. We were a couple of big-timers, sitting there in the lap of luxury with our beers and Swisher Sweet cigars. In truth, I was a little nervous about drinking my first beer, but I was also thrilled and in no way a panty-waist. I screwed the top off nonchalantly, as if I were a coal-miner about to knock back a cold one at the end of a long, hot day. I felt Mark's eyes bearing down, so I didn't hesitate in taking a drink, which was easily the worst-tasting thing I had ever put in my mouth, and I summoned all of my will to keep my face from registering my utter disgust and disappointment. I had wanted to love beer, and I hated it.

"Well, what do you think?" asked Mark.

"Good beer," I said immediately. "Tastes better than out of a can."

When he wasn't looking, I poured most of the beer into a nearby potted plant. Still, during my adolescence, I had more evenings such as the one described above than I care to remember, especially when I read about teenagers actually dying from binge drinking. The other day, a friend of mine remarked, "You know, we were just lucky to survive our teenage years."

Yeah, we were. I don't know how we made it. I can't even remember how we got that Nova out of the cornfield.

CHANGES

She is frail and withdrawn, having been beaten back into the recesses of her own bruised body, so far back that when she speaks, her voice echoes in some empty chamber inside her, an emptiness that grows larger and more profound each day. She has forgotten what it feels like to be a whole person; that has been taken from her, too, her memory of better times, when love seemed not just possible but palpable, growing inside her first as an idea, then as an actual connection with another person, and finally as a child, which seemed to her the miraculous culmination of all her dreams. Romance, marriage, family...once upon a time she sat in classrooms, gazing out windows or doodling in her composition notebook, shaping gangly schoolboys to these designs, matching her name with others to see how it felt. And it felt remote. Could such a thing ever be hers? Was there a man among these boys, one who would know her when he saw her, one who would love her always, tender and sweet, one who would never let her go and never let her down?

She cannot fathom now how she ever saw him in such a glow, nor can she recall the excitement she felt on their first date, or the moment when it became clear to her that this man was the one she had been waiting and hoping for all her life, the one in songs she heard on the radio, the one who rescued those troubled women in the books she read.

That man, she feels certain, never existed except in her fantasies. Or if he ever did exist, he died the night that this other man, a stranger in her husband's body, slapped her face for burning dinner. The slap left only a welt beneath her left eye, but it killed her husband, the one she loved and married, the one who fathered her child. He was gone forever.

Oh, he pretended not to be dead. He'd come out later, climbing into this stranger's skin and assuming a familiar role. It was like one of those people you see on TV who impersonates celebrities. Her husband had a talent for imitating himself. Gestures, mannerisms, pet names. It was uncanny, but she was not fooled. Her husband was dead, and now she belonged to this other guy. Was this what she deserved for being so gullible, for believing in "destiny," for marrying someone whose special qualities no one else could see? Wasn't that how love worked anyway: You see what no one else can? What was it that she had seen? She can't remember.

A couple of times after it started, she left. But it was hard, admitting she had been wrong, hard admitting it to her family and friends, even harder admitting it to herself. And it was hard to face a future she could no longer trust. Hadn't she proven that she had no judgment? This new man in her life told her she was stupid, sometimes before he hit her, sometimes after, sometimes — if she was lucky — instead of. Well, maybe she WAS stupid. Maybe she could find someone to protect her from the stranger, but who could protect her from herself?

Then there was the burden factor. It was humiliating to come crawling to other people for help. She thought she could maybe figure a way. He might get tired of her, or maybe God would come and either change him again or kill him once and for all. Sometimes she pictured a boulder falling on his head, like on those Bugs Bunny/ Roadrunner cartoons.

She'd leave, but she wouldn't stay gone. She was afraid of him, but she was more afraid of what was left for her in this tired, old liar of a life. Somehow, she felt responsible for this mess. She knew she shouldn't — people told her it wasn't her fault, but she couldn't help how she felt. Anyway, she believed she had learned how to tiptoe around him at certain times, avoid him altogether at others. Plus, she was always devastated when her daughter asked about her daddy when they did leave.

What is she supposed to do? She enrolls in college. One of her teachers encourages his students to keep a journal as a way of clarifying problems in their lives. She writes a few things, things that make sense, maybe. Maybe she can...oops, better go, here he comes...

SHOWER CURTAINS, PUTTY KNIVES

As you well know, there are only two more weeks before Christmas, which means there are 13 more shopping days, giving me roughly 10 more days before I will begin my annual crazed-guy-on-a-gift-buying-binge shopping spree. Some people — and you know who you are — spend the entire year thoughtfully and methodically purchasing Christmas gifts for their loved ones. Sometime in March, when I am just beginning to reckon with the holocaust of my charge cards from Christmas past, these dear hearts are picking up nifty little items just perfect for a particular friend or relative.

"Oh, look, honey — wouldn't Aunt Louise look spiffy in that monogrammed hunting vest?"

Those of you who buy gifts year round, I hate you for it, I really do. By now, your Christmas shopping is done, long since. All you have to worry about, with your cards already in the mail and your twinkling lights strung with perfect precision along the hedgerow, is keeping fresh water in the tree stand so the needles don't dry up, since you've had your tree up for several days now and won't take it down until New Year's Eve. I once had a pet hamster that didn't live that long.

I, on the other hand, will select my tree about five days before Christmas, passing on the bundled up trees in front of the stores since I will no doubt want to capture the true essence of Christmas by cutting my own tree. I'll find a little tree farm, where I'll choose among the picked over trees some mutant, a forlorn, horribly misshapen thing with pathetic branches, something that looks more like a squid than a Christmas tree. But I'll love it just the same, more even, and I'll decorate it with what few ornaments I have, and lots of tinsel, lots and lots, until it resembles not a squid, but a squid with very shaggy silver hair, and my guests will remark, "Good grief, son, why don't you put some more tinsel on that poor thing!"

Then, my heart full with what I've done to animate my home with the Christmas spirit, I'll be off on that shopping spree. It may well be that you have had time, patience, and consideration on your side in choosing gifts for your loved ones. I say that's no match for spontaneity and pure adrenalin. When you have 64 hours to buy 16 gifts, it gives you a rush like no other. The downside of last-minute shopping is that all the "hot" gifts are already long gone, and "hot" gifts, of course, are what people want, your relatives included. In such cases, I have found it wise to fall back on the practical. One Christmas, for example, I couldn't find a Malibu Barbie for my seven-year-old niece, so I got her a putty knife and a shower curtain, one with tropical fish since she's a kid and all. You should have seen the look on her face when she opened her gift. Pure Christmas.

I learned a long time ago that it doesn't make any difference what I get for my dad. I used to spend a great deal of time pondering what to get for him, and over the years I've tried everything from electric razors to tennis rackets to ball caps that read, "If the trailer's rockin', don't bother knockin'." Yet, in the intervening years, I have never seen my father shave with that razor, play any sort of tennis, or wear any kind of hat, not even those featuring clever couplets.

Then, a couple of summers ago when I was staying at his place during a brief vacation, I stumbled upon a cardboard box, which contained—are you ready?—all the Christmas gifts I had bought for him since 1973. The tennis racket, the Rubik's Cube, the razor, the hat, the gloves lined with rabbit fur, the Hai Karate cologne and after shave, four packs of baseball cards, and other suchlike—it was a treasure trove of junk and memories, symbolizing at once the power of simple objects to bring the past alive and the utter futility of finding useful gifts for those you love.

I say, go with the putty knife.

BORN SINNER

By the time I was eight or nine, I knew I was going to hell. I knew because the preacher of our small Baptist church said that all those who had not been saved would surely wind up there, swimming in a lake of fire forever, and I had not been saved. I knew because many of my cousins and friends had gone to the front of the church during altar call, weeping marble-sized tears of remorse for their sinful lives, while I stood there praying not for my soul — which I could not fathom — but for an end to the service, an end to the intermittent glances of relatives who were hopeful that this would be the week I'd come to the Lord and join the church.

But week after week, year after year, I resisted, without really understanding why. Maybe I was afraid everyone in the church would see through me and know I wasn't really saved, even if I pretended really hard. I was sure God would know, just as he must have known that many times, right in the middle of the most sacred hymns, my mind was occupied not with salvation, but with the way a rebellious ray of sun can render even a Sunday-go-to-meeting dress translucent. As I mouthed the words to "Amazing Grace," I tried desperately to fight off the lewd images Satan had planted in my brain. The battle of heart versus hormones, I'm afraid to say, was not a very long one, nor was the outcome ever very much in doubt. I couldn't really pray for those thoughts to leave my mind because, in truth, I really didn't want them to (except in uncomfortable situations like church or gym class), and I didn't want to lie to God about it.

So I stayed a sinner. I was a born sinner, the preacher said, and every week I refused Christ, my heart would get a little harder until, finally, I would run out of chances. On the other hand, I could, at any time, get killed in a car accident, and if I had not been saved, I would burn forever and never see any of my loved ones again.

My parents had been saved and baptized together when they were married. I had seen pictures of them in the river with two preachers, all of them up to their knees in the brown, muddy water. For some reason, the pictures made me feel bad. I had been to a few baptisms, and they always made me feel bad. People cried, and sang in off-key, nasally voices, and the people who were being taken into the river always looked afraid, as if they were scared they might drown. I know that I always felt queasy when the preacher said that the new members were being "washed in the blood of Christ."

At some point, all of this came to an end. I don't remember how it happened—I just didn't have to go anymore. And what a welcome reprieve it was—no more fear, no more anxiety. I found that I had, over the course of time and many altar calls, rejected my entire family's religion. I discovered I did not really believe that people who worshiped differently from us were going to hell, and I did not believe unsaved eight-year-olds were going to hell if they died in car accidents, and I did not believe a lot of other things I heard every week. At the same time, however, I did find myself believing in God, and Jesus, and the promise of eternal life. I hadn't rejected religion altogether; I just couldn't accept any religion predicated on fear, or on a "we're right/they're damned" philosophy.

Maybe that's what I was rejecting all those years ago—the high-pressure tactics of the well-meaning.

OOH, THAT SMELL

Though I recognize their vital contribution to the world and am thankful for it, the truth remains that I do not like hospitals. I do not like being in them. I do not even like seeing them on television. ER may be a great show, but I'll never know. Somehow, the very idea that millions of viewers are crowding around the set every week to watch a team of fictitious surgeons operate on somebody's fictitious spleen is repulsive to my delicate sensibilities.

Which is to say, I'm squeamish. For me, the smell of gauze is nauseating; the prospect of a tetanus shot is enough to inspire an anxiety attack. The hospital is a chamber of sensory horrors. It's akin to taking a boy who has a fear of chocolate on a tour of a Hershey's factory. In a hospital, a squeamish person is constantly under siege, his senses flooded, drowned in an ocean of gauze.

Recently, a close friend of mine was hospitalized, and I paid him a visit, trying to suppress my admittedly irrational feelings about hospitals and making a pretty feeble effort to cheer him up. He was going to have a "procedure" performed on him later in the day which would involve an instrument that looked like a missing part off a '71 Chrysler.

The procedure would, of course, be medieval in nature, requiring heavy medication and a healthy suspension of disbelief ("You're going to put that WHERE?"). He was going to be drugged.

It occurred to me that many of the patients must be drugged before they are actually admitted. How else to explain their apparent willingness to don such degrading, cruelly tailored attire? Have you seen these outfits? They have a papery texture and are rather, er, airy in design, quite revealing but hardly becoming. If Calvin Klein had turned in such an outfit in one of his freshman fashion classes, he would have been given an 'F' and told to change majors.

Why must the outfits be so humiliating? Is it, as a colleague suggests, an effort to create a classless society of patients, a sort of socialism of the tacky? Or is it more utilitarian—those trying to escape would be easy to spot and certainly subject to immediate arrest if caught outside the confines of the hospital in such a costume.

In any event, the patients must be drugged to the point of hallucinating before any effort is made to get them to put the things on: "Oh, Mr. Fields, you look simply dashing in this blazer. It makes you look 10 pounds lighter and 10 years younger!"

Another thing I noticed is that rooms apparently are now

equipped with a rubber glove dispenser. I saw one right there on the wall next to the door. To me, this seems just a little bit crass. Can't the staff bring their own gloves, or are the dispensers there just in case a visitor gets a sudden, inexplicable urge to probe the patient himself? For a moment there, I felt like I was in the bathroom at the Texaco.

Luckily, my friend made it out of the hospital and is back on his feet. Now comes the part for which no amount or caliber of drugs can prepare you — the bill. That's enough to make anybody squeamish. Say, were those hospital outfits monogrammed?

LUCKY STRIKES OUT

When I was a kid, there were few things in the world I liked more than to watch my dad play poker. I liked the way he held his cards, so familiar, as if they were extensions of his own fingers, and I loved the way the men bantered back and forth, some refusing to watch their language, which made me feel like part of the fraternity even though I was just 11 or so. I was amazed that anyone could win — or lose — a hundred dollars and never change expression; to me, such nonchalance was unimaginable. But perhaps above all other things, I loved the way the players smoked cigarettes.

Each player had his own particular style of smoking, as distinct as a signature. One player held his cigarette between his thumb and forefinger as though it were a bug he was afraid might get away. He drew on it hard and long, the lit end burning bright orange for several seconds at a time, and there was kind of a sizzling sound. When he exhaled, the smoke poured through his nostrils. It reminded me of a dragon.

My father, of course, had the coolest style. He seldom touched his cigarette, which instead dangled from his mouth as if it were alive. The cigarette seemed of a piece with him, moving up and down when he talked and hanging inanimate when he was still, studying his hand. When he did speak, to crack a joke or place a bet, the smoke continued to come out of his mouth right along with every word, even if it was a longish sentence. For some reason, I thought this was marvelous — a smokestream of words.

It was my own father who first made smoking seem so glamorous. Then there was Thomas, a neighborhood boy a couple of years older than I who had developed quite a reputation as a troublemaker and who had the added appeal of having been held back a year in school. During the summer, when he got bored, he'd come by with a couple of other suspicious-looking characters and we would go down into the woods behind my house, where he'd pull out X-rated magazines featuring girls who seemed as remote as astronauts. We would look at the magazines until we got bored and decided to go fishing.

But one day, Thomas brought something else. Cigarettes. Menthol. He pulled one out of the pack and self-consciously tapped the filtered end against his finger before lighting it. He had been working on his nonchalance, but wasn't quite there yet. Still, I was very impressed. Then he offered me one. At last, my time had come.

I was going to smoke. I was going to dangle the cigarette from my lips while I talked and blow smoke through my nose and grow up and lose a hundred dollars on a full house without batting an eye. Suddenly, my future was all laid out in front of me like a picnic.

I took the cigarette and held it in my hand as though it were a holy thing. I tried to think of different ways of holding it, wondering if all the styles were already taken. I put it in my mouth and immediately felt about 10 years older. I pictured myself in the smoking area at our high school, hanging out with the guys from shop class, telling lies about cheerleaders. Thomas held his cigarette against mine, lighting it. I gagged instantly.

"Don't worry, Cox," he said. "You don't know how to inhale yet."

It was true; I didn't. I wasn't even sure what it meant. I liked the cool, almost minty taste, but I couldn't seem to swallow the smoke as Thomas instructed, and I was enormously disappointed with the way the smoke just burst out of my mouth all at once, before I could even get two words out. I tried and tried until I felt dizzy, but I was just not getting it.

"You're not smoking," Thomas said. "You're just puffing on it like a girl."

It was a judgment. Thomas was right. I wasn't a smoker, would never have my own style, would never lose a hundred dollars playing poker, and would never, under any circumstances, be welcome in the smoking area. Oh sure, I tried on my own for a few weeks to learn, but I just couldn't get the cigarette to become part of me, felt even more awkward than usual trying, and finally gave it up entirely. Lucky strikes out.

Now, everyone I know who smokes would like to quit. My father still plays poker and still smokes, even after three heart attacks and a triple bypass. Several of my closest friends swear they would give anything to quit, but can't seem to shake it. I wanted desperately to smoke and couldn't; they want desperately to quit and can't.

I'm not sure what happened to Thomas, but if he's still out there, he's probably still smoking, and not like a girl either.

DOES THIS PUNISHMENT REALLY FIT?

There always seems to be much ado about just how lax and ineffective our criminal justice system really is. Do you remember, for example, the great hue and cry over the caning of that young American spray-painter in Singapore? Evidently, many people feel that this is a sensible form of punishment.

The upshot appears to be as follows: why aren't we caning our criminals over here, instead of letting them play ball and watch reruns of the Flintstones on cable all day, and why on earth don't we execute more people, maybe at noon on Fridays at the town square?

My question is, do we really need to turn to violence as an antidote to an increasingly violent society? That's like solving the problems of one alcoholic by getting everybody else drunk. "It's OK, Burt—you may not be getting much better, but who's gonna notice anyway?"

Kneejerk liberal, you're thinking, bleeding heart, soft on crime, soft in the head. But you haven't heard my solution yet.

Shopping.

That's right. If we really want to nip crime in the bud, we've got a foolproof way right underneath our noses; not only will it cost the taxpayers nothing, in the long run it will save millions as we reform potential career criminals before they have a chance to get started.

I envision it this way: two young boys out on the town, busting up mailboxes, spray painting people's cars, and worst of all, playing heavy metal music at a volume that would rattle china cabinets in the next county. They're caught, brought to trial. If it's in Singapore, they're likely to lose a couple of fingers or get some unneeded dental work. If it's the United States, suspended sentences, probation, and maybe a stern lecture from a sour-faced judge.

Why not shopping?

"Son, for your crimes against your fellow citizens, I sentence you to the following: eight hours of continuous shopping at the department store of your mother's choice. If you do not have a mother, one will be appointed to you by the court. You are to try on a variety of starchy clothes that don't fit and in which you will look like a complete geek, and you can expect to be stuck by a number of hidden needles.

"Also, you will attempt to refold the clothes exactly as they were before you tried them on, and you will then endure the snide looks and remarks that are certain to follow as the sales clerk grabs the merchandise from your hands and says, 'Here, I'll do that.'

"Further, you will spend at least one quarter of your sentence observing your mother in various outfits that SHE wants to try on, and you will nod approvingly and not look bored when she asks you if this is her color or if this one makes her hips look slimmer.

"At no time are you to sneak away to a record store or an arcade, and at no time are you to sit down, unless it is for the purpose of trying on Argyle socks to go with your turtleneck and blazer. If you fail to live up to any part of this, the length of your sentence will automatically be doubled."

Not bad, huh?

My plan will work for two key and indisputable reasons. Number one, most violent criminals are men. Number two, men hate to shop. It begins in early childhood, when our mothers make us try on shirts and khaki pants until we start feeling like mannequins. Dead, but handsomely dressed.

This horrific ritual is repeated at least twice yearly, once at Christmas and again on the Saturday before school begins, and usually lasts all day.

Part of the promise of graduation is that we'll never have to shop again. We've earned it. Then we learn something else. Either we outgrow our clothes, they become embarrassingly obsolete (leisure suits, for the man who likes to play!), or they simply and literally come apart at the seams. Now what?

Shopping, that's what. Only we do it a slightly different way, left to our own devices. Here is our method: Buy the first thing that fits. If it comes in different colors, buy several, to prolong the amount of time before we'll have to shop again. It's a very basic, sound principle.

Let's face it. A man will wear the same five pairs of underwear for twenty years before he'll spend one precious second of his ever-dwindling life in Belks looking for the latest in leopard-spotted briefs. Fine. But if he crosses that line, he ought to pay. Real time. Hard time. Trying on slacks. Talk about your cruel and unusual punishment.

THE SEARCH FOR FAITH

One of the most popular short stories in my literature classes is Nathaniel Hawthorne's "Young Goodman Brown," the tale of a man whose suspicions of the inherent evil nature of humankind are so great that he ultimately loses his faith one evening on a mysterious journey into the forest. He enters the forest a "good man," a good Puritan (the story's setting is around the beginning of the 18th century, near Salem), but reappears later a paranoid, utterly faithless man destined to live out a life of misery, loneliness, and doubt.

Students enjoy debating whether Brown's dark view of human beings is distorted, the result of his own weakness, or just unflinchingly realistic — maybe people really are essentially bad; maybe that's why we need laws and rules.

There is also almost always a lively discussion about faith. Is it a specific religious faith that Brown loses in that forest, or is it something else, perhaps faith in his fellow human beings or maybe faith in himself? Students rarely agree on this point, but one thing they invariably agree about is that Brown does lose faith in something and that it is this loss that dooms him.

On the day Timothy McVeigh blew up that government building in Oklahoma City, many of us could recognize Young Goodman Brown's struggle as our own. We came home that evening and turned on our television sets and our screens were filled up with images of blood-streaked survivors — and non-survivors; terrified mothers screaming for their missing children into a sky vast and empty beyond the billowing smoke; weeping police officers, trained to protect and to serve, able to do neither, just more helpless people running around in no particular direction because the carnage was in every direction.

The bomb sheered off nearly half the building, killing dozens, maiming dozens more, and traumatizing an entire nation.

Maybe, like me, you had a hard time watching the footage. The sight of unalloyed despair and suffering is not easy to endure. And then come the old, familiar questions. Why? How can such a thing happen? How can anybody be so evil? How can God, any God, permit such violence to be visited upon the innocent?

How can we continue to have faith in a world in which such arbitrary, seemingly meaningless, excruciatingly painful acts occur? Well, there is no easy answer, at least not for me. Like Young Goodman Brown, I struggle mightily with such questions. I look through the television and into the eyes of a young mother who has just lost her two children and husband in the terrorist attack and I look for hope, and I look again. What meaning does hope have for her? How would she define it now? What are the charred remains of her faith?

There are people who will say that it is God's will and must not be questioned, and there may indeed be angry letters to this effect arriving shortly after this column's publication. But it is not God I question, but myself. Can I find my own faith in the rubble? Can I survive these little doubts that crop up in my heart like weeds in unseen corners of the yard?

Most of us have had experiences with grief, pain that must have seemed impossible to bear. We have survived the loss of loved ones, many gone far too soon and for no good reason we could know of. We have been betrayed by those closest to us, friends, husbands, mothers, lovers. We have experienced personal failure and wondered whether we had it in us to go on, whether one capable of such weakness had the character to make it, even deserved to make it.

And so we enter the forest and wrestle with all of these devils that would deceive and destroy us. Our faith is challenged, again and again.

I have seen the faces of the defeated, heard the moans of the faithless, who are certain that the world is out to harm them, that people cannot be trusted, that they themselves have little of value to offer. Locked inside the world's pain, they turn on the things they once held as immutable truths — the essential value of life itself, the belief in a higher power, the goodness of people. And little by little, day by day, hour by hour, they waste away, no longer hungry for the food of life, no longer able to stand the taste.

But some do survive with their faith intact. Some even manage to locate a stronger faith, a faith not based on hand-me-down, untested dogma, but on something profoundly felt, something found unexpectedly in the deepest, darkest corner of the soul at the peak of its crisis.

Because, underneath the rubble, underneath the anguish, underneath the cancerous doubt, there is faith. Whether it is faith in a higher power, faith in each other, faith in one's self, or some combination, it is there.

Among the world's countless dead and dying, though it is buried now and then, in the carnage in Oklahoma City, in the carnage of our own lives, faith survives, waiting to be rescued. We must never stop looking for it.

CALL THE MAN

There is just one thing I dread about going home for Easter, and that is seeing a certain relative. It isn't that I don't get along with the guy. In fact, there is only one reason why I can't really stand being around him. The thing is, he's handy. That is, he's always fixing things, or making little improvements. Every time you see him, he's painting or paving or adjusting or sawing or planting or building something. His whole life is a series of little handy verbs.

I, as you may have already surmised, am not handy. I realized I would never be handy early on, in 4-H camp, when I was about 10 or 11 years old. Each day, we were supposed to make these crafts, such as potholders and ceramic shakers and little wood and tile jewelry boxes. The other kids seemed to get the knack fairly easily, producing reasonably attractive and completely functional gifts for their soon-to-be proud, beaming mothers and fathers. I, on the other hand, produced items which no human could ever identify and for which there could be no conceivable function. My key accomplishment was avoiding injury around the sharp tools used to create my grand abstractions. In retrospect, I'm sure they would have fetched a whopping price at modern art shows, but why look back?

The point is, I was no good with tools, could find no purchase whatsoever on the road to handy, which so many have traveled. For many years, my self-esteem suffered. In high school, while friends of mine were souping up their cars with their dad's tools, I had to go to the service station to get someone to replace my windshield wipers. In college, while my friends were rigging their television wires so they could get free cable — including HBO — I resorted to a coathanger and tin foil (once again: modern art!) so I could see one blurry channel, which seemed to show nothing but reruns of "Eight is Enough."

Now, I am reconciled to the fact that I will never be handy. I will not be retiling my bathroom this summer, or putting on a deck, or painting my car, or even replacing a few cracked windows in my house. I will not be in Lowe's Hardware, which must be heaven for the handy, unless it's to buy some light bulbs or something equally simple. I have nothing against Lowe's — it's just that being around so many handy people at once makes me utterly neurotic, even at my advanced state of self-actualization.

I think the main reason that those of us who are not handy feel anxiety around people who are handy is that many of them simply do not understand our handylessness. For them, it is a sign of low character, a certain laziness, perhaps a manifestation of latent communism or, worse, prissiness. Handy people are always wanting to look at our hands, checking for tell-tale signs of smoothness, softness.

Handy people look at us with disdain; I know they do. They bait us, asking questions about our cars and houses and yards and workshops (as if!), sneering if our answers reveal our handy-cap.

"You mean you'd actually hire someone to paint your own house, when you could do it yourself? If I threw away money like that, I couldn't look at myself in the mirror every morning. But maybe that's just me..."

Yes, it is. I can say so because I have reached a state where many of my kind never arrive. I know I'm not handy and never will be, so I just go with it. If I need something painted or paved or fixed or adjusted in any way, I simply call the man (or woman, as the case may be). I do not, as some poor fools do, deny my lack of handy skills and forge ahead, trying to do it myself, in order to prove a point. Usually, the point that is proven is that we non-handy people will eventually, inevitably pay approximately twice as much to the truly handy to undo the mess we've created than we would have had to pay to start with.

What, I ask you, is more pathetic than a non-handy person trying to do handy things? Maybe just one thing: a handy person painting tiny green shutters on an orange birdhouse or, better still, explaining the entire process, step by step, to you while the kids hunt for Easter eggs, delirious in their oblivion.

I'M ALLERGIC...NO, REALLY

I do not like cheese. I have never liked it. In fact, I hate it. The smell of it makes me ill. The very thought of it is repugnant to me.

You are probably thinking, so what? He doesn't like cheese. Big deal. Well, I agree with you. So what? Big deal. If I don't happen to like cheese, that's my problem. It's certainly not the end of the world. It's hardly a ripple in the swimming pool of life. But the fact is, people seem to have a problem with my not liking cheese. Many take offense. Others have a hard time believing it. Some demand an explanation.

For example, if I am with a group of people in a restaurant and we decide to order a pizza, I can't really go in on a family-size with anyone else since I eat my pizza without cheese. When I mention this, my fellow diners are invariably incredulous. It's as if I'm up to something, and they can't figure out what.

"C'mon," they say. "You can't eat pizza without cheese. It isn't natural. You can't even taste the cheese. How can you do that? It's un-American."

Suddenly, my dislike of cheese is treasonous. Under such circumstances, I am obliged not only to explain why I don't like cheese—even on pizza—but to defend my patriotism as well.

"Well, I can taste the cheese," I say. "Besides, did you know that Thomas Jefferson didn't like cheese on his pizza either? And Abraham Lincoln would not eat a grilled cheese sandwich. That gets left out of the history books because of the powerful cheese lobby."

Once, when I was ordering a pizza in a restaurant in Atlanta, the waitress actually refused to take my order to the cook. I ordered a pepperoni, sausage, and mushroom pizza with no cheese, and she just couldn't seem to accept what I'd done.

"You're not serious, are you?" she asked. "I'm not sure we can do that."

Probably a town ordinance.

"What does a pizza with no cheese look like? I bet it looks awful. I wouldn't eat it. Why don't you just try it with cheese just this once? You're in Atlanta."

Yes, I probably would love Atlanta cheese, whereas the Carolina cheeses make me nauseous. It's geographical.

I'll make a confession. At a certain point in my life, I grew so weary of fending off the unwanted advances of cheese lovers who were so anxious to win me over or else simply understand my peculiar ways that I resorted to outright lies.

"I'd like a Canadian Bacon pizza with onions, green peppers, and no cheese."

"No cheese? But..."

"I'm allergic," I'd cut in, interrupting their challenge before it even began.

And that did it. I discovered that while people are perfectly willing to challenge your tastes, few will bother confronting an allergy. Still, there is that curiosity to contend with.

"What about milk? Can you drink that? How about ice cream? Cottage cheese? You poor thing."

Though I basically agree with the old saying that honesty is the best policy, I continue to bend the rules a bit when it comes to cheese. It's a bit like telling your aunt that she looks simply marvelous in her new polyester jumper. You may not actually believe it, but consider what you'd be getting yourself into by being completely truthful.

Let's face it — she looks terrific in her new outfit, and I'm allergic to cheese. We can all live with that, can't we?

MALE PATTERN BALDNESS: LET IT BE

PART ONE: Portrait of the Artist as a Young Man.

As a youth, I had a head of hair that was the envy of every woman who ever cut it. Women cut my hair because I grew up during the 70's, when hip young men wore their hair quite long and savagely blow-dried, and the male barbers in my town just couldn't quite catch up with the times.

When you're thirteen, haircuts are beyond crucial. They are defining moments. A good one can be your ticket into the right crowd. A bad one can mean social exile, alone in the cafeteria, munching on your chuckwagon sandwich at the same table as the crowd that wore brown socks in gym class.

I suppose hairstyles were so important to us because they were the one thing about our appearances over which we maintained at least some control. The rest of our physical features depended on the mercy of forces beyond us. I, for example, was so skinny that even my closest friends referred to me as "Famine Man," my own mother accused me of having no butt, and the local druggist used to offer to buy me lunch every time I came in to buy a magazine and Clearasil.

Many other kids had it no better. Some had a large nose, or ears, some were a bit overweight, some struggled vainly against acne, some wore braces, thick glasses, some zoomed into puberty too soon, and some straggled in late.

So hair was more than important; it was sacred. And mine was gorgeous, blond and lush, spilling over my ears and on past my collar, or piled up wet into the greedy hands of the local beauticians, who cooed things to me as they shampooed.

"Ooh, honey, if I had hair like yours...I know two dozen women who would kill for it. Do you know what women have to go through with their hair, and then you prance in here with a head like this one? Ooh, wee!"

PART TWO: Portrait of the Older Man as an Artist

I could, even in those halcyon days, look at both sides of my family and see it coming. I saw the advertisements on television. I saw the anxious looks that worked their way into the faces of young men not long out of college.

And I saw art. I saw the artistry of the common man. I saw that necessity was the mother of invention and that death was the mother of beauty and that hair spray was one mother of an accessory.

I saw the balding man.

I saw him in the form of my father, whose once proud black locks had begun to betray him just as my blond ones reached their full glory. Oh bitter irony! I saw in our bathroom closet a dazzling assortment of tonics and gels, and I found clogged in our bathtub drain the remnants of all their broken promises. Pinched between my thumb and forefinger, it resembled something the cat might've coughed up.

I saw a thousand and one comb-overs, heaven help us, and these in varying degrees of success. Some were tastefully done, others less so. Some were plainly bad art, the hairstyle equivalent of the dogs-playing-poker painting.

A couple of these still survive today. One, which I will call the Industrial Strength Comb-over, involves the usual sweep of long hair from one side of the head to the other, covering the naked cap at the peak, with the added feature of about one keg of hairspray, so that what results doesn't so much look like hair, but a piece of metal.

This particular style should come with the following warning for those who wish to use it: "WARNING—The Surgeon General has determined that the Industrial Strength Comb-over may be dangerous to anyone who attempts to run her fingers through it and could even be fatal to the wearer in the event of strong winds, when the thing tends to blow straight up like some kind of lid or car hood, then slams back down with devastating force. Also, there is the ozone layer to consider."

Just as bad, perhaps, is the dreaded Swirl. This is a variation of the Comb-over in which the wearer combines whatever long, anarchist strands remain into one mighty force, then proceeds to wrap the so-called "superstrand" around the top of the scalp in a kind of swirling effect. The potential danger here is that if the job is not done with extreme care and artistry, then the result might look something like an ice cream cone, or an upside down mini-tornado.

Also, if viewed from above, this style might induce dizziness and/or nausea.

Now, men, I have come to join you in this futility. Here in the 90's, I can find no woman who envies my hair, which features a hairline receding so fast I feel I can almost see it moving. And, yes, I try to wear it in such a way that its gradual departure is somehow less apparent.

But I say it's time to stop the madness. To paraphrase the Beatles, let it be, man. Throw those gels and tonics into the junk heap, along with your application to the Hair Club For Men and your toupee brochures. Lighten up on the special effects and gimmicks, and give the hairspray a rest.

Let it be, let it be.

"WHY DON'T YOU CALL BROOKE?"

"Got a girlfriend yet?"

My dad, speaking on behalf of the entire family, is concerned. I have been back in the dating pool for seventeen long months now, and still no girlfriend. I think some of them are worried that I may mope around the house in my bathrobe until I'm about 47, then marry some teenager from the Philippines.

I tell my dad I'm playing the field, that I'm writing my memoirs, that I'm working on home improvements.

"Field my eye," he said. "You're laying around on Friday night eating Chee-tos and watching that medicine woman on TV. You're not old enough to have any memoirs, and you couldn't build a birdhouse if you had a kit. You need to get out some. Lillie thinks you ought to court Brooke Shields. I think if they can put a man on Mars, you ought to be able to take a girl out to Shoney's."

I remind Dad that there's not a man on Mars, just a camera taking some snapshots. And I tell him to give Aunt Lillie the bad news about Brooke Shields: She's married to a balding tennis player. I won't be bringing her home for Thanksgiving after all.

I suppose the family has a right to be concerned. For months after my separation, I did, in fact, mope around the house quite a bit, accomplishing important, life-affirming tasks such as memorizing the weeknight lineup of *Nick at Nite* and playing my electric guitar at an excruciating decibel level, which I hoped was loud enough to compensate for the fact that I can't play and can't sing. I am to the guitar what Pauly Shore is to acting. Still, I wrote angst-ridden songs in the manner of "Love Stinks," "Love Hurts," "Love is a Battlefield," and the ever popular "He Stopped Loving Her Today," in which the protagonist's only escape from the torments of love is death. I wasn't good enough to play these particular songs, however, so I wrote songs such as "I Hate Love," "Your Love is Like Rancid Milk," and my personal favorite, "Love is Worse Than Rabies," in which the protagonist's only escape from the torments of love is to die from the bite of a rabid skunk.

My friend Bill, also recently divorced, has been going through the same permutations. We call each other regularly, sometimes to whine about how hard it is to meet women, sometimes for a badly needed confidence boost. We've gotten pretty good at propping each other up with inspirational comments such as, "You the man!" and "Go get 'em, tiger!"

Just this weekend, Bill came up from Charleston, and we charged into Asheville Saturday night looking to break hearts, he in his crisply pressed blue shirt and beige trousers, me in my ultra-hip Miles Davis tee shirt and jeans. We went in a little dance club called Cinjades, and, right away, I saw three very attractive women, all in very fetching black dresses. One of them even looked at me, though it may well have been my ultra-hip Miles Davis tee shirt that did the trick, and I immediately notified Bill.

"Well, why don't you talk to her?" he said. "You're supposed to be some sort of writer, aren't you? Surely you can string together a few words. Look at you. An English professor who works out, with his own house and own car and two very handsome dogs. And you're wearing a Miles Davis tee shirt. Who's cooler than you, WHO? You the man!"

Thus inspired, I waited for the woman who had looked at me to pass by — I didn't want to seem too eager — while I rehearsed some VERY clever opening remarks. When she passed by, I was still rehearsing.

"That was a good one, man," said Bill.

"Yeah, well, if she looks at me one more time, that'll be my cue. Then we'll know it's meant to be. I'll be ready then."

And just maybe I will be, since I'm the man and all. Of course, if I'm not, I could always wait around until Brooke Shields leaves that runty tennis player. Anything for my Aunt Lillie.

RADICAL YOUTH

It is National Poetry Month, and I am thinking of Suzi, a girl who moved into town and changed my life when I was a high school junior. She was a complete oddball, with chopped off hair, a collection of weird cassette tapes of bands I'd never heard, and a skewed view of the world that I found utterly compelling. For her, the only appropriate reaction to an insane world was insanity, and she seemed to flirt with it like a cheerleader flirts with a quarterback. She dressed like a hobo, draped in sweatshirts two sizes too large and ragged jeans ripped every which way. She was perpetually unkempt, a genuine spectacle among all the girly girls who were forced to spring out of bed at 5 a.m. to sculpt their hair with curling irons, rollers, sprays, and other accoutrements of the perfectly coifed. After all, it was the decade of Farrah, for goodness sakes.

Suzi, of course, cared neither a fig for Farrah, nor any of the legions of girls who tried so hard to emulate her. She was into Karl Marx, baby, and Carl Jung and Walt Whitman. Not exactly Charlie's Angels, not likely to appear on some eighth-grader's lunch box, or a poster in the boys' locker room, but she adored them all the same.

She was always reading, before, after, and even during class. She was the first person who taught me that rebellion does not necessarily have to be self-destructive. Like her, I despised the whole idea of school and most any other institution you can think of, from the church to the Campfire Girls. We believed all of them existed for the sole purpose of controlling our minds and turning us into good little John and Jane Q. Citizens, with toy poodles, picket fences, fixed mortgages, Veg-O-Matics, and one week a year in Myrtle Beach. We hated all that. Let the preppies have the American Dream. We were going to wear camouflage to the prom and write strange, incomprehensible poems on the back of our graduation programs. We were going to sabotage all experiments in biology class, wear homemade T-shirts protesting team sports, and use the school's activity bus for non-school-sanctioned "activities."

Until I met Suzi, I never really had much use for poetry, except as a method to placate teachers who were angry because I hadn't "applied myself," or "worked to my potential." Though I had no use for John Crowe Ransom, I had a knack for hanging rhymes, and most of my English teachers took this as a sign that they had inspired something in me. In reality I loathed the routine of reading assigned poems and forming an occasional idea, only to have it shot down by some teacher who believed her B.S. at Western Carolina automatically rendered her interpretation superior and infinitely more sophisticated. The last thing I wanted was for some teacher to serve up poems like riddles to be solved, then explain the "answer" as though there could be no other.

I wrote poems, of course, and kept them in spiral journals under my bed a few respectful feet away from the Playboys. Suzi was the first person I ever permitted to read a poem I had written that actually mattered to me. She gradually introduced me to thrilling new writers that were not to be found in any of our school anthologies, writers such as Tom Robbins and Richard Brautigan, the author of *Willard and His Bowling Trophies* and other classics. I became fascinated with Brautigan's poetry, in particular, which was completely different from anything I'd ever seen. His poems included such things as werewolves, Ferris wheels, Kool Aid, and electric teardrops. Brautigan wrote the kind of poetry no teacher can ruin, the kind that is impervious to academic dissection. He was the first poet that I ever truly loved, because I felt he was speaking to and for me. He reopened some doors I had closed and, lo and behold, in walked a host of other poets: Whitman, Neruda, Yeats, Dickinson, and many others.

When my literature students tell me, on the first day of class, how much they hate or "don't get" poetry, I always just urge them to hang on, that there's a poet coming; one they will recognize as all their own, with messages just for them. Hating poetry based on one or two bad experiences makes no sense — it's like tuning in a Michael Bolton song on the radio and declaring, "Yecchh! I hate music!"

Poetry is not just for teachers, and it is not just a series of inscrutable riddles. Suzi understood that, and she helped me understand it. She was, like any other visionary, years ahead of her time.

THE CAR THAT ATE ITSELF

It all begins with an ungodly sound. Metal on metal. The sound of some drunk fool trying to cut his cheating girlfriend's Ford Escort in half with a chainsaw. The sound of a fork and a spoon trying to gnaw their way out of a beer can. The sound of two tractors making love in a Kansas cornfield under a harvest moon.

But I know it is none of these things because I have heard this sound before. I heard it almost exactly one year ago at a time when you would least like to hear the sound of shrieking metal — when I was driving home from work. It began gently enough, not really even as a scraping sound, but more of a good-natured rattle, which you might reasonably expect in an eight-year-old Toyota. I thought it gave the car a little bit of personality, maybe a sort of "lived in" feel, like an old house with creaking wood floors or cabinet doors that don't quite shut. You know, kind of pleasant, even rhythmic. Oh, you, chitty chitty bang bang, chitty chitty bang bang, we love you.

Unfortunately, this phase did not prove lengthy. Within a short while, the sound became less hypnotic and more assertive, nudging rudely into my consciousness, forcing me to reckon with it, compelling me to turn down my blaring tape deck and pay rapt attention. It is that dreadful moment when you realize that something is actually wrong, seriously wrong, and it's not going away. Mechanics are going to be in your immediate future — their faces suddenly appear there on the windshield like some vision in a crystal ball — and, wait a minute, now you see a checkbook, and five weekends in a row at home watching "must see TV" because there aren't that many places you can go with the change you scoop up from underneath the couch cushions. Or is it, god forbid, the Visa or MasterCard that you see?

As the sound of scraping metal morphed into the hellish noise of an engine eating itself, I knew I was soon going to get to live the great American dream of maxing out a major credit card. And that's exactly what happened. I guess it was a bad sign when I pulled my car into the mechanic's parking lot, and all the mechanics came out at once to see what was making all the racket. When I got out, they were all shaking their heads in unison, like dancers in some terrible off-Broadway musical.

Bottom line: My car had thrown a rod, and my entire engine had to be rebuilt to the tune of $2,400. Oh well, it had been a good car these eight years, and the fellows told me if I let them rebuild the engine, I would probably be able to drive it another 100,000 miles at least. So I went through with it, making the good folks at Visa very happy indeed with the interest I would be paying for approximately the next 38 years. Still, as the fellows pointed out, at least it would be cheaper than buying another car.

That is assuming, of course, that I would not hear any more of that wonderful metal machine music for a very long while. So you can imagine how I felt last week when I was tooling down the highway listening to the Rolling Stones' ominously titled album "Let it Bleed" and a very slight tap-tapping commenced out of time with Charlie Watt's drumming. "Gimme Shelter," indeed.

This time, I knew the drill. I was as sensitive to my car's engine as a mother is to a newborn's cough at 2 a.m. I immediately wheeled her into the mechanic's shop, to the same fellows who rebuilt my engine the year before. The initial prognosis was a loose bolt, but the next day when I arrived to pick her up, the mechanic was shaking his head again. I had seen that shake before, and I knew the news was going to be bad.

Broken crankshaft. Major repair job. Several hundred dollars. I could feel my own insides grinding now, the gears of my heart stripped bare. I was stunned. The mechanic seemed sympathetic and said he'd try to help me out as much as he could. Once again, my future is in his hands. Maybe I'll get a break. Then again, maybe I've got a lot of pork and beans to look forward to, and many gripping episodes of "Suddenly Susan."

Maybe the best things in life are free, but everything else costs a fortune. That thought occurred to me Sunday as I walked two miles to the grocery store. You have a lot of time to ruminate on such things when your car's in the shop. And not only is walking good exercise, but there is very little chance you'll hear that gut-churning metal on metal sound. Give me raspy breathing any day. It's a lot cheaper.

REQUIEM FOR A CLOCKMAKER

Three weeks ago, my grandfather slipped as quietly and easily into death as a leaf slips over the lip of a small waterfall. Alzheimer's had already taken most of him in torturously slow increments over the past ten years until there was nothing much left but a pair of opaque, uncomprehending eyes and a body that resembled nothing so much as a crumpled dollar bill left alone on a table. When he died, he had been in the rest home for almost five years.

One of the preachers at his funeral was once on the *Tonight Show* back in the days when Johnny Carson was still the host. The preacher had become kind of famous for his uncanny ability to spell words backward. You could say, "delicious" to him, and he would instantly respond, "S-U-O-I-C-I-L-E-D," just like that. The first thing Johnny Carson said to him was, "So you're from Sparta?"

"A-T-R-A-P-S," said the preacher at once to the befuddled Johnny.

The preacher did not spell any words backward at the funeral, but he did mention how he had always been fascinated by my grandfather's ability to put together a clock and make it work. I had been fascinated, too. As a child, I thought he must be some kind of magician, somehow able to conjure time from a shiny sprinkle of dust at his fingertips, little cogs too small to tell apart with the mortal eye. His workshop was also magical, with dozens of clocks of every conceivable size and description situated in every nook and cranny. There were clocks everywhere, and on the hour, they all chimed in unison, like a bunch of kids clamoring for attention, one trying to be heard above the others.

For nearly fifty years, people brought their fractured clocks to my grandfather, and he put them back together. Toward the end, before Alzheimer's stole that magic from him, he might have taken several weeks to get to a job, but people didn't care. They knew he could fix it, and they were willing to wait.

Then there was the music. For him there was only one kind — old-style bluegrass. He could play the guitar and the banjo, and he loved to record sessions with his picking buddies on an old reel-to-reel tape machine, particularly if they had had a drink or two. Later on, most of these tapes were transferred to cassette, and I still listen to them from time to time, even though the sound quality is not all that great. Back in the 1960s, a couple of guys from the Smithsonian showed up at his farm one day wanting him and his buddies to play some songs for a record they were making. My grandma thought they were probably frauds, but Papa got the guys together and they did record some songs that are now part of a collection in the Smithsonian Museum. They even sent him a copy.

He did love music, but his tastes were not as broad as they were deep. My Aunt Sandy used to drive him nuts playing Elvis upstairs in her bedroom, and not too many years ago my grandma brought home a tape of Randy Travis, who is considered by some to be the best country music singer of this era. Papa watched the tape machine without a word until the music went off, and then proclaimed, "Well, if that's country music, I'm a Baptist preacher."

Well, my grandpa was many things — a clockmaker, a musician, a gun collector, an animal lover, a voracious reader, so many things that 750 words can never get at — but he was no Baptist preacher. He did, however, scare the devil out of us children from time to time. Until very late in life, he utterly loathed the television, and we were terrified he might catch us watching it. He never struck any of his grandchildren, but he was once an imposing figure, over 220 pounds, and he had a gruff temperament at times. He also believed that children should be obedient; he wasn't much given to the more modern modes of child-rearing, which stressed communication and nurturing over discipline.

But old age softened him considerably, and as I entered my late teens and early twenties, I was amazed at how sweet he had become, and how talkative. He'd entertain us for hours with wild stories about his travels out west, and his terrific sense of humor became increasingly apparent. He couldn't play music anymore — arthritis had gnarled his hands, and his knuckles were almost as big as golf balls. But he could still entertain.

Then came, in succession, the death of his only son in a freak accident, the onset of Alzheimer's, and the slow disintegration of a proud, great man, a man who once courted his future wife by singing his favorite song, "The Rose of San Antone" on their first date.

I hope he's singing it right now and that if Elvis is singing, too, it's down the hall a ways in some other part of the mansion.

SUING MOM

Edward Shlikas had had enough. As a law student at Wake Forest University, Shlikas had been subjected to so much abuse in the classroom at the hands of his professors that he began to lose weight, suffer from "debilitating headaches and fatigue," and fall into depression. It seems that Shlikas' professors expected the 28-year-old student to answer questions in front of his classmates. Can you imagine!

As a savvy law student, Shlikas wasn't about to let Wake Forest and its professors get away with such atrocious classroom practices. After all, there would seem to be a pretty good chance that such behavior might eventually lead to actual tests — written, multiple choice, whatever — in which Shlikas could conceivably be called on to produce evidence that he had learned something about the course material. The very idea!

Faced with such impossible circumstances, Shlikas did all he could do. He filed suit against the university. He's suing for more than $125 million in damages. In the court of public opinion, Shlikas is probably already a loser, but I can understand where he's coming from. I can feel his pain. Yes, I, too, was once involved in a lawsuit some skeptics might find questionable.

My story begins innocently enough, with a junior varsity basketball game, but it winds up not on the basketball court, but in a court of law, with three siblings suing their own mother. I should know. I was one of the plaintiffs.

During the game in question, it began to snow heavily, leaving the roads slippery and treacherous. On the way home, my mother simply could not make a sharp turn at the bottom of a fairly steep hill, and we plunged into a river. By the time it was all over, she had been through an incredible ordeal, having experienced the sight of her children banged up considerably and on their way to the hospital in an ambulance. She must have had nightmares of the steering wheel that just won't turn, and I'm sure she felt tremendous guilt over the accident. The question was, what could we, the family, do to help ease her pain?

The answer, of course, was to sue her for negligence. That's right, negligence. It turns out that she *could* have chosen another, perhaps safer route from the high school to our home. That was going to be the crux of our case against her. She should have known better, and because she exercised such poor judgment, putting all our lives in danger, she was going to have to pay dearly.

Or, rather, her *insurance company* was going to have to pay dearly. At least that was my father's logic. For years we had paid these outrageous premiums, only to get the runaround when a claim had to be filed, and now our ship had come in. Of *course*, the lawsuit had merit—good, honest, hardworking people and their kids don't plunge into rivers unless God wants to get even with an evil insurance company.

For the record, though we ultimately persuaded my Mom to go along with the plan—what choice did she have, after all, as the defendant—I do not believe her heart was ever really in it. But my brother, sister, and I were ready. I, for one, had seen the future, and it had a red Camaro in it. After all, I was on the verge of getting my learner's permit. God was on our side. Pretty soon, Nationwide would be, too. My Mom's brother, who just happened to be a lawyer ("fate," said my dad), even signed on to represent us.

We felt confident going into court, perhaps too confident. I was the first of the three siblings to be called to the stand. My uncle, the attorney, had warned us that the insurance company's lawyer would try to pick at our emotions, and he had coached us on what to say. I held up fine, and so did my sister, who turned out to be a fairly poker-faced twelve-year-old. Then came my brother, Jeff, age eight.

"So, young man, you blame your own mother for hurting you? You're claiming the woman who clothes and feeds you, the same one who carried you in her womb for nine months, the woman who tucks you in at night and lets you sleep in her bed when you have nightmares or it thunders outside, this woman is guilty of NEGLIGENCE?"

There was a brief pause, followed by a quivering lip, then a trembling voice, then a full-throated cry which pierced all the hearts in the courtroom: "Nooooooo!!!"

My brother sobbed on the stand, which I immediately surmised was not a good sign for our case, an intuition that was affirmed first when I looked at my sister, who was also crying, and finally at my father, who was crying perhaps hardest of all.

My brother's a good fellow, but he's certainly no Edward Shlikas.

MERRY CHRISTMAS

I can't say that I really understood the true meaning of Christmas as a child, but I knew that Christmas Day meant more to me than anything. My parents tried to teach me what Christmas was actually all about, both by explanation and by taking me and my younger brother and sister to church on Christmas Eve, where the birth of the baby Jesus was sung about, discussed, and finally portrayed in touchingly inept dramatic performances put on by stage-shy, gangly kids trying their best to act sincere while huddled around the real star of the show, a forty-watt light bulb wrapped in swaddling clothes.

When you're eleven-years-old, dressed up in sheets and towels from your mother's linen closet, loaded down with frankincense and myrrh, and stranded on stage in front of pews and pews of doting adults, it is not easy to remember your lines, much less to pretend that the savior of the world was manufactured by General Electric. Even Marlon Brando would have a hard time being convincing under such circumstances, particularly if his mind was dancing with visions of sugar plums, Tonka trucks, and ten-speed bikes.

But even if I did not fully comprehend the miracle of Jesus' birth and the implications of the resurrection, I sensed that Christmas was special for reasons other than all the neat stuff kids got every year. Of course, that was special, too. For most kids of my generation, the real bible was not the King James version, but the Sears Christmas catalog, which we received sometime in October or November and read out of every night with enormous reverence, circling "passages" and formulating heartfelt prayers that we might, on Christmas Day, experience the miracles promised herein. Praise Sears, from whom all blessings flow?

Once the stress of the play was over with, we could all finally begin counting the hours to Christmas morning. Before we left the church, one of the church members, usually somebody's uncle, played Santa, passing out little paper bags filled with miniature chocolate bars, Hershey Kisses, candy canes, and an orange or a tangerine.

"That's not really Santa," some kid would whisper conspiratorially. "It's Mr. Sneed. See the way his feet point out?"

"I know," I'd say. "Anyways, Santa's probably in Mexico or somewhere by now."

We had all seen the weather reports before, and we were familiar with the way Santa's progress could be tracked on the Doppler radar. "Better get in bed, kids!" the weatherman would tell us. "Santa's on his way." And, sure enough, there were Santa and his reindeer on the Doppler radar, moving across the Atlantic Ocean at an alarming speed, much faster than any hurricane ever could. Well, I thought, what do you expect from a fellow who visits sixty million households in less than eight hours?

Then we'd hurry off to bed, curl up in little balls, and try our best to sleep. Of course, we would not be successful, at least not until sleep caught us off guard and took us in spite of ourselves. Until then, we lay there in the utter stillness of the dark, monitoring every sound, real or imagined, fashioning images of Santa stealing across the rooftop, his footfall muted by the snow. Then a terrible thought: How could he possibly fit a ten-speed bike down our chimney? Because, you doubting moron, Santa has more power than is dreamed of in your tiny philosophy. He owns Sears, for crying out loud.

Needless to say, it has been quite a few years since I experienced the rush kids feel on Christmas Eve, but I haven't forgotten it. And I am satisfied with the tradeoff, now that I understand that Christmas is more about the healing power of love and forgiveness than the excitement of a new toy. Or maybe it's just that, as our dreams get bigger, the meaning of Christmas must expand to accommodate what even Sears cannot provide: the possibility of redemption, and miracles more lasting than a ten-speed bike.

BEANPOLE

I should have been a girl.

At least, that's what I used to hear as I was growing up. I heard it a lot. I heard it from relatives and strangers, teachers and coaches, friends and adversaries, all of whom took one look at my willowy body, deep brown eyes, and thick, wavy blonde hair and decided God had somehow gotten it wrong. It was as if I were a two-headed pig, more suitable for the carnival than grade school.

"Gather 'round, ladies and gentlemen, and see the boy in the girl's body. Isn't he pretty?"

By the time I made it through my second growth spurt sometime around my freshman year in high school, I hated my body more than anything else in the world, with the possible exception of a handful of older school bullies who liked to trap me in the hallway or playground and make me say my name, since I had a lisp and was cursed with a name full of 'S' sounds.

"Now what's your name, little girl?"

"Chrith Coth," I said to peals of instant laughter. The bullies, who were some of the most popular guys at our school, would punch each other in the arm and make me say it again, maybe two or three more times before letting me go. "Chrith Coth."

"Well, hello, Chrith Coth. You better run along now and play with your dolls."

Eventually I got speech therapy and more or less cured my lisp, but there was precious little I could do about my body. As a freshman, I was almost the same height I am now—6'3"—and I weighed 123 pounds. With almost no flesh on me, my long, narrow bones protruded so sharply into my skin I looked like a bag full of coathangers. My arms and legs dangled like wind chimes from my torso, which seemed little more than a rib cage and shoulder blades draped in a thin blanket of skin. I wore heavy sweaters and sweatpants under my bluejeans to give the appearance of more size, but it was pointless. "Here comes Famine Man," one of my friends used to say.

But I was far from famished. In fact, I ate at every opportunity, and I ate things that are supposed to guarantee weight gain. Ice cream by the gallons, peanut butter, junk food, spaghetti—if it was considered fattening, I devoured it. But my metabolism was so high that my body was like a furnace, burning every calorie I sent its way.

147

At night, I would pray to God to help me. All I wanted was to be normal, with just a regular body like everyone else. I didn't want to be a girl, and I didn't especially care about being in the gifted class. Was it supposed to be compensation that I was smart, when all I really wanted was not to be so skinny? In those days, I would have traded my spot in the gifted class for a pair of decent biceps without a moment's hesitation.

I gradually did gain a little weight, but not much. By the time I graduated high school, I weighed about 150 pounds. It's been a few years since then, but it is fair to say that I have never been able to overcome my insecurities about my body image. Perhaps it's my childhood, or maybe it's our culture's emphasis on physical appearance above all else, or maybe it is quite purely and simply a character flaw. I would love to tell you that I've overcome such self-indulgence and have at last learned the valuable truth that we are not our bodies — instead, I must admit that I spend an average of 12-15 hours per week in the gym in an ongoing effort to exorcise the demons of my past.

And, for better or worse, I have changed my body over the past few years. I now weigh about 220 pounds and have become the envy of many a high school junior, all of whom seem to be filled with questions about how long I've lifted and the training methods that have enabled me to add approximately 100 pounds to my once gangly frame. In some ways, I believe I have developed a kind of reverse anorexia — no matter how big I get, I sometimes still see a skinny boy trying to catch up. But not always. Sometimes I see a grown man prepared at last to deal with the bullies. Then I feel sad all over again. After all these years, I'm finally confident enough for grade school.

THE PROFESSOR AND THE BUNNY SLOPE

Because of a disproportionate need for approval that can doubtless be traced back to some childhood trauma, I tend to fall in love too fast and often say yes when I would rather say no. When these two tendencies intermingle, the results are invariably toxic, as they were a few short months ago when I suddenly and inexplicably found myself on a pair of skis.

Having been born and raised in the mountains, I have been around skiing and skiers all my life and had, until this year, always found myself utterly indifferent to the whole shebang. Skiers, with their ruddy faces, chapped lips, and slightly runny noses, have always seemed to me like some alien race recently arrived from the planet J. Crew. All decked out in their gaudy-colored wool and Gore-Tex suits, absurd headgear, and too-cool-for-school mirror shades, most skiers are about as interesting to me as a wilting head of lettuce. And though I know I'm being irrational, I've always felt there was something slightly narcissistic about those ski racks on the tops of the Volvos and LandCruisers you see on the interstate. "We're going skiing, and you're not!" they seem to say as they blow past you on I-40. "We're part of something you'll never understand."

And I couldn't understand it. How many times had I seen that poor fellow on the Wide World of Sports — you know the one, the "agony of defeat" guy, airborne one moment, a heap of mangled limbs at the bottom of a hill the next. Why would I want to take a chance on winding up like that guy?

Because Pam was going, that's why. On the strength of one lunch date and a handful of friendly conversations, I was suddenly ready to abandon all of my instincts about skiing. Some of my friends at work had been trying to get me to go for quite some time, and I had consistently resisted. But not this time. Pam was going, and so was I.

On the way to the slopes, my friends warned me that I might ought to take the time to get a lesson, or spend a few hours on the "bunny slope" until I could get my bearings, but I scoffed at these suggestions. 1 was a grown man, I figured, with an impressive athletic pedigree. Suddenly, I was bursting with confidence. Had I not made honorable mention all-conference in tennis my senior year in high school? Had I not, as recently as 1984, won the 4-H putt-putt championship in Sparta, NC, where memories of my historic birdie on the crucial 17th hole still linger, though the windmill has since been torn down and the whole course paved over?

No, I would not be wasting any time on the bunny slope with the prepubescents. 1 would strap on my rented skis, get on the chair lift, and head to the top with the others. I would experience the thrill of victory. I would summon my long dormant athletic prowess and master this course before we broke for lunch, and Pam would clap her hands with delight as I carved crisp, symmetrical patterns on the way down. These were the thoughts I had as one of the college boys who worked there helped me figure out how to attach my skis to my blue neon moon-boots.

As it turned out, there were two obstacles in this scenario. Number one, Pam didn't show up. She'd had a minor emergency and had to change plans. There would be no delighted hand-clapping, then. And number two, once I finally reached the snow, I found that I could not stand up at all unless I remained perfectly still on a perfectly flat surface. The very instant that I made any attempt to move even one centimeter, my skis went immediately out from under me and 1 was flat on my back. I felt like a character in some old black-and-white slapstick comedy, maybe "The Professor and the Bunny Slope" or something, and the entire earth was suddenly one giant banana peel.

Unfortunately, getting back up proved as difficult falling came easy. I discovered that simply standing up required a complicated strategy that left me in several impossible positions. The world then became a game of Twister, with the right hand on yellow and the left foot on green, hamstrings stretched taut as a ship's sail in gale-force winds.

In time, with the help of extremely patient friends and after at least a dozen failed efforts to move, I finally did make it to the chair lift. The remainder of the day is too ugly to recount here, too graphic for sensitive readers and too depressing for the author to recreate. Suffice to say, events unfold inexorably toward a hot bath, a family-size tube of Ben Gay, and a bruised humility that can only be brought about by the agony of defeat.

Heaven help me if I ever meet a woman who's into bull-fighting.

WEDDING PICTURES

I have always liked to look at pictures of brides. The first thing I do when I buy the Sunday paper — in any town — is turn to the section where the brides are and linger there like a gardener in reverie among his fragrant rows of perfect flowers. They are beautiful, all of them in the fullest bloom. There is nothing in their aspect that suggests winter will ever come — they seem to believe they will wear these same faces forever. I don't know if this is faith or innocence, but I am delirious for it. I do not want to pick them for my own, but admire them where they are.

I like to read their names and scan the paragraphs that tell about their lives, and I love reading between the lines. This one was graduated from Wake Forest and just began a new job, while her new husband is in his last year of law school. They will have to get by on her paycheck until he gets out of school. Maybe they'll live in some cramped, noisy apartment for awhile, but they'll soon be looking at homes in nice neighborhoods and talking about color schemes. They got married at Lake Junaluska and will live in Winston-Salem after spending their honeymoon in France.

And here's a middle-school teacher with 16 years in already — the proverbial late bloomer. Her husband is the co-owner of a landscaping business. They will honeymoon in Jamaica and make their home in Candler. She's known a little disappointment, maybe, and had resigned herself to the small satisfactions of freedom weighed against ever encroaching loneliness, which was assuaged just a little by a good book, or a walk around the school's athletic track in her new Reeboks, or the simple passage of time, or nothing at all. Then she met him at a party she almost decided not to attend because she had a hint of a headache. Now, when she's asleep, he rolls her ear lobe between his finger and thumb, feeling the texture of small moments, and her dreams of contentment deepen.

The wedding announcements in the Sunday paper tell us everything and nothing. Embedded in these plain descriptions are the amazing, preposterous, and altogether wonderful stories of life. Here, for all the world to see, are people willing to take an awful chance. Haven't they been warned by all the losers in love, haven't they seen the startling statistics, don't they know the odds are against them? Don't they know, from their own experience, that even if they don't wind up hating the other person, this bloom is bound to wither, that rapture will give way to a complacency the familiar makes inevitable? Does she not believe that he will sometimes take her for granted when she needs to be prized? Won't he, from time to time, forget something important? Will she, now and then, catch him looking one moment too long at a younger, firmer woman?

This land is cluttered with the rubble of divorce, and it makes many of the survivors hard. People who stay together too long "because of the children," then using them as weapons, surprised at themselves in rare moments of self-awareness. People whose lives are derailed when it is not only their partner's eyes that wander off the track. People who live day to day with the haunting suspicion that they are wasting their lives on someone who can never really fathom them, while there is someone waiting out there who can.

I have a friend who likes to repeat the old cliche that "love is a misunderstanding between two fools." Marriage, then, must be the ultimate foolishness. Just a few weeks ago, my brother was married even as he was surrounded by divorce. My father and mother, my sister, and yes, me too, all victims. Divorce runs in our family like some mutant gene. He is a fool and his new wife a flower, pushing up toward the sun through dirt not fit for growing, her beauty somehow more extravagant for this stubbornness.

I am a fool, too, I know. I still believe in marriage, even though I know very well the pain of failure and the calamity of loss. Of all the muscles in the body, by far the most resilient is the human heart, no bigger than a fist. Divorce can turn the heart into a fist, I guess, angry and violent. But, now and then, when I see this woman or that woman, I catch myself wondering what she would look like in profile, in the Sunday section, and I feel the fist of my heart opening one finger at a time, reaching out, maybe, ready to touch someone, maybe, and be a little foolish once again. Or maybe a lot foolish.

May I always be such a fool.

ACKNOWLEDGEMENTS

Of course, this book would not have been possible without the cooperation of several newspapers, most prominently the Waynesville Enterprise-Mountaineer and the Asheville Citizen-Times. I thank both newspapers for giving me permission to reprint these essays. I am particularly grateful to Scott McLeod, editor of the Mountaineer, for giving me lots of room during my tenure with his newspaper.

I am even more grateful for a supportive network of family and friends, who must suffer the slings and arrows of outrageous fortune when I am moved to write about them in any given week. So I am compelled to mention my parents, James W. Cox and Margaret Crouse, as well as my brother, Jeff, and sister, Lisa. I will save mention of other family members and friends for later.

Though our marriage did not work out, I must devote a paragraph of thanks to my former wife, Carole Finger, who was not only supportive of my writing throughout our relationship, but was a fabulous sport from start to finish. We all have our foibles, but not many of us are willing to read about them in the paper. Carole never made me feel as if I was invading her privacy when I wrote about either her or our marriage. Instead, she always believed that I was destined to make it as a writer, even when I didn't believe it. Hopefully, someday I will be able to justify this faith. In the meantime, the debt I owe her for this confidence and support cannot be overestimated. She is a remarkable person, and I continue to hold great affection for her and her entire family.

Obviously, I owe much thanks to all the readers, particularly those who have gone out of their way to let me know they enjoy my work. I have been incredibly lucky in this regard. I am especially grateful to have met Dr. Terry Nienhuis, who teaches English at Western Carolina University, and Ms. Connie Withers, a retired lady with a sharp wit and discerning eye. It was the two of them who finally convinced me this book might actually be a good idea. Without their encouragement, it is unlikely I would have followed through. I appreciate and admire them both.

On the technical front, I owe a considerable debt to Anita Burgin, one of my fellow teachers at Southwestern Community College. Anita has helped guide me through the labyrinth of computer file conversion and solved any number of problems that might have killed, or at least seriously delayed, this project. I would also like to

Chris Cox

thank the staff of Parkway Publishers: Michelle Lakey, assistant, for editing, and Julie Shissler and Robin Ann Aylor, for editing and book design. Many thanks to Bill May, Jr. for his cover design.

Finally, I would like to acknowledge Ron Coulthard, one of my former professors at Appalachian State University. I had a number of great teachers at ASU, but none taught me as much about writing as Dr. Coulthard. While I'm at it, I would like to express my deeply felt appreciation to the entire English department at Appalachian State. My stay there marked a significant turning point in my life, and I am indebted to a number of my teachers for their tremendous influence.

I want to thank the following individuals for their help, support and inspiration:

Stewart Royall, Owen Gibby, Glenn and Wendy Gray, Tim Perri, Bill Danaher, Elgin and Lillie Atwood, Louise Evans, Kate Cox, Stephanie Worley, Edwin T. Arnold III, Michael Wagoner, Michelle Keilen, Jean Ellen Forrister, Mary Hartman, Cheryl Contino-Connor, Renee Cohen, David Shiek, April Gladden, Marsha Lee Ball, Michael Revere, Connie Shuler, Monroe Gilmour, John R. and Evelena Cox, Adam Wyatt, Katelyn Wyatt, Pete Sansbury, Joe Barwick, Mrs Reeves Betts, Terry Presnell, Shawn Poole, Stephanie Worley, Edwin T. Arnold III, and all my friends at the Haywood Regional Health and Fitness Center and Southwestern Community College.

154

Waking Up in a Cornfield
by: Chris Cox

The Critics Say

Now and then a piece of writing comes over the transom that is so nearly perfect in its way that I read it with a sigh of admiration mixed with envy. If Chris Cox were not a writer, he would be a painter or a musician. He has a lovely sense of the music and color of words. -- *James J. Kilpatrick, Syndicated columnist, The Writer's Art*

Whether it's two boys drunk in a cornfield or memories of a dying grandfather, these short essays are uncommonly funny, poignant, insightful, and compassionate. Chris Cox is one of the best undiscovered writers in this genre in America today. -- *Terry Nienhuis, Professor of English, Western Carolina University*

Reader's Comments

At last, a fresh, young voice — a wonderful writing style, and a variety of thought-provoking subjects. My friends and I had a weekly ritual of finding out what Chris had to say. -- *April Nance, Asheville*

For years we looked forward to reading the columns of Lewis Grizzard. We may not have always agreed with him, but he made us think. Then death took him from us. But we still had Mike Royko. We did not always agree with him, but he, too, made us think. Now death has taken him from us. But we still have Chris Cox. -- *Doris O. Howell, Robbinsville*

My husband and I eagerly await your weekly column, and are of the opinion that it should be syndicated. -- *Naomi Bastow, Hayesville*

Thanks for the wonderful columns you are writing. Keep up the good work and know that you've got a whole lot of folks who need to hear your message! -- *Monroe Gilmour, Black Mountain*

I miss Lewis Grizzard so bad that I never thought I'd like to read anyone's column again. But you have me hooked sure enough. And I sort of have a little crush on you, too. After all, you are as cute as a speckled pup. It's too bad I'm old and married and have grandchildren. I'm glad to know we have talent such as yours in these mountains. -- *Jan, Robbinsville*

Please continue your columns because I believe you could go nationwide. Perhaps you could become a twentieth century Robert Ingersol. This country needs you. -- *Claude Lacouture, Franklin*